The *Reformation Heritage Bible Commentary* is a unique series that promises to be a valuable resource for laity and preachers. The verse-by-verse commentary focuses on major topics, providing clear interpretation and devotional insight in keeping with how the Reformers approached Scripture, and emphasizing themes that were central in their teaching. Illustrative quotes from key Reformers and their heirs, including Lutheran, Calvinist, Anglican, and Wesleyan sources, provide insights in their own words, without trying to survey the range of views represented in this heritage. This focused approach gives a clear reading of the text which engages one's mind and heart.

—The Rev. Dr. Rodney A. Whitacre
Professor of Biblical Studies
Trinity School for Ministry
Ambridge, Pennsylvania

Busy pastors and teachers of the scriptures need commentaries that are biblical, theological, and practical. Fortunately, the present commentary on Colossians and the Thessalonian letters fulfills those requirements. In addition, the commentary is accessible to a wide variety of readers, for it is written in a wonderfully clear way. I commend this work gladly.

—Thomas R. Schreiner, PhD
James Buchanan Harrison Professor of New Testament
The Southern Baptist Theological Seminary
Louisville, Kentucky

This was not a ponderous tome to be endured; it was an opportunity to monitor a lively seminar. As leader, St. Paul places on the table church doctrines, heresies, and challenges. These topics are then discussed by the minds and pens of Luther, Melanchthon, Hus, Cranmer, Chemnitz, and others. It was a joy to hear them and a comfort to find their struggles and successes are mine.

—Pastor Ken Klaus
Speaker Emeritus, The Lutheran Hour

If the commentary on Colossians and I and II Thessalonians is indicative of the entire series, the *Reformation Heritage Bible Commentary* promises to be an asset to the library of serious Bible students, whether layman or clergy. This series exemplifies the reformers commitment to sola scriptura, that the revelation of God's saving purposes is in scripture alone, which is primarily about Christ alone. The blend of overviews and insights from our protestant forefathers with exegesis and application from contemporary reformed theologians makes for an interesting read. Contemporary readers will also appreciate the devotional notes in these commentaries. Because the study of God's word is not just an academic endeavor, it engages the mind, heart and will of those who trust Christ for their salvation. While many modern commentaries seem to focus on the application of the scriptures, the intent here is gospel centered interpretation, resulting in devotional application. This is a work of serious scholastic intent combined with theological scrutiny and integrity. I am grateful for such a work and confident that it will be profitable for years to come in aiding the church's effort to know Christ more fully as He is revealed in holy scripture.

—Kenneth R. Jones
Pastor of Glendale Baptist Church, Miami, FL
Co-host of nationally syndicated talk show – White Horse Inn
Contributed to: "Experiencing the Truth", "Glory Road", and
"Keep Your Head Up"; all published by Crossway.
Contributed to Table Talk and Modern Reformation magazines
Frequent conference speaker

The Reformation of the church brought with it biblical insights that revitalized churches and radically changed the course of theological studies as giants like Luther, Melanchthon, Calvin, Chemnitz, and Wesley commented extensively on Holy Scripture. The new *Reformation Heritage Bible Commentary* is a one-stop-resource where the observations of these and other distinguished Reformation leaders are brought together around specific books of the New Testament. This first volume in the series, *Colossians/1 & 2 Thessalonians,* is an impressive treatment of these Pauline letters that pastors, laypeople, and professional scholars will treasure and find eminently useful.

—The Rev. Dr. R. Reed Lessing
Professor of Exegetical Theology and
Director of the Graduate School
Concordia Seminary, St. Louis, MO
Member of the Society of Biblical Literature,
the Catholic Biblical Association, and
the Institute of Biblical Research

This first volume of the *Reformation Heritage Bible Commentary* proves itself to be a useful resource for pastors and laity. The brief modern commentary focuses on the key features of each verse. Also, references are interspersed throughout the commentary to the great reformers and to the creeds of the Reformation. The results are illuminating and theologically informed.

—David W. Chapman, PhD
Associate Professor of New Testament and Archaeology
Covenant Theological Seminary

COLOSSIANS
1 & 2 THESSALONIANS

Reformation Heritage
BIBLE COMMENTARY

✦ COLOSSIANS
✦ THESSALONIANS

EDWARD A. ENGELBRECHT

PAUL E. DETERDING

CONCORDIA PUBLISHING HOUSE • SAINT LOUIS

Library of Congress Cataloging-in-Publication Data

Engelbrecht, Edward.
    Colossians and 1 & 2 Thessalonians / Edward A. Engelbrecht and Paul E. Deterding.
        p.   cm. — (Reformation heritage Bible commentary)
    Includes bibliographical references and index.
    ISBN 978-0-7586-2771-1
    1. Bible. N.T. Colossians—Commentaries. 2. Bible. N.T.
    Thessalonians—Commentaries. I. Deterding, Paul E., 1953- II. Title. III. Title: Colossians
    and 1 and 2 Thessalonians.

    BS2715.53.E54   2012
    227'.077—dc23   2011044778

1   2   3   4   5   6   7   8   9   10   21   20   19   18   17   16   15   14   13   12

Contents

About This Series   ix

Acknowledgements   xiii

Abbreviations   xv

Timeline for Paul's Letters   xix

Maps   xxii

     Paul's Missionary Journeys   xxii
     Colossae and Asia Minor   xxiii

Colossians   1

     Introduction   3
     Part One: Preaching (chs. 1–2)   9
         The Image of God (Article)   22

         A Shadow of Things to Come (Article)   46

     Part Two: Paul's Instructions (3:1–4:6)   51
         The Prison Epistles and Persecution (Article)   62

     Part Three: Conclusion (4:7–18)   65

1 Thessalonians   71

     Introduction   73
     Part One: Greeting and Thanksgiving (chs. 1–3)   77
     Part Two: Exhortations (4:1–5:22)   107
     Part Three: Conclusion (5:23–28)   131

2 Thessalonians   135

     Introduction   137
     Part One: Greeting and Thanksgiving (ch. 1)   141
     Part Two: Exhortation and Encouragement about the
         End Times (ch. 2)   151
         The Reformers on the Topic of Antichrist (Article)   156

     Part Three: Apostolic Commands (3:1–15)   165
     Part Four: Conclusion (3:16–18)   173

ABOUT THIS SERIES

The great reformers' influence upon the Bible's interpretation and application could not help but revitalize our churches. This is as true today as it was 500 years ago. This renewal happens in part because the reformers drew upon the insights of the Renaissance, which linked the medieval church back to her earlier roots in the ancient world. There the biblical texts sprang up. The reformers were among the earliest students to pursue classical studies, not only due to personal interest but especially due to the benefits such study brought to the study of the Bible. By reading the New Testament Scriptures in their ancient languages and context, the reformers dispelled many misunderstandings.

Second, the fires of controversy, which followed Luther's proclamation of justification by grace through faith on account of Christ alone, served to refine the study of Sacred Scriptures. So many ideas that medieval people took for granted or that were accepted based on human authority alone were tested and retested, leading to more careful study of God's Word.

Third, the reformers themselves taught with special insight due to their constant reading, study, translating, and preaching of the Sacred Scriptures. Their approach to the Scriptures and the insights they gained have continued to inform biblical studies even to the present day. For all of these reasons, Concordia Publishing House wished to produce a readable commentary series that would serve the current generation by sharing with them (1) insights from the reformers and (2) commentary that stemmed from their heritage.

In preparing this commentary, we drew upon the insights of the following reformers and heirs to their evangelical approach to teaching the Scriptures:

John Hus (c. 1372–1415)	John Knox (c. 1513–72)
Martin Luther (1483–1546)	Martin Chemnitz (1522–86)
Thomas Cranmer (1489–1556)	Johann Gerhard (1582–1637)
Philip Melanchthon (1497–1560)	Johann Albrecht Bengel (1687–1752)
John Calvin (1509–64)	John Wesley (1703–91)

Not every commentary in this series will include quotations from each of these reformers since these authors did not all comment on Books of the Scriptures with equal frequency. Other reformers may be included, as well as citations of Reformation era confessional documents such as the Augsburg Confession and Westminster Confession. Readers should not conclude that citation of an author implies complete endorsement of everything that author wrote (heaven knows, these were fallible men as they themselves acknowledged). The works of other significant Reformation era commentators are less available in English. We have intentionally stayed away from more radical reformers such as Andreas Bodenstein von Karlstadt, Ulrich Zwingli, Thomas Münzer, etc.

The commentary is not simply a compilation of sixteenth century views but a thorough verse-by-verse commentary built from the reformers' approach of *Scripture interprets Scripture* and supplemented from their writings. Along with quotations from the reformers and their heirs, readers will also find quotations from some early and medieval Church Fathers. This is because the reformers did not wish to overthrow the earlier generations of teachers but to profit from them where they were faithful in teaching the Word.

Some readers will note that the writers listed above represent different branches in the Protestant family of churches, and they may wonder how compatible these writers will be alongside one another. It is certainly the case that the reformers held different views, especially concerning the Sacraments, biblical authority, and other matters. Some authors for the series may at times describe differences between the various reformers.

However, while it is true that these differences affect the fellowship and work of the churches of the Reformation, it is also true that the reformers shared significant agreement. For example, the great historian Philip Schaff noted, "Melanchthon mediated between Luther and Calvin" (*History of the Christian Church* vol. VII, second revised ed. [New York: Charles Scribner's Sons, 1894], 260). Early Reformation works like Melanchthon's *Commonplaces* and the Augsburg Confession served as models for the various traditions of Protestant confession and doctrine. What is more, as the writers focused on a particular biblical text for interpretation, they often reached very similar conclusions regarding that text. The text of Scripture tended to lead them toward a more unified expression of the faith. This is something I have described as "the text effect,"[1] which illustrates for

---

[1] *Friends of the Law* (St. Louis: Concordia, 2011), 136.

us a way in which the Bible brings us together despite differences and always remains the most important guide for Christian teaching and practice. In view of the 500th anniversary of the Reformation in 2017, I believe it is fitting for us to draw anew upon the time honored insights of these great servants of God.

The Bible Translations

Among the translations for our commentary we have chosen, on the one hand, what many regard as the finest English translation ever produced: the King James Version. The KJV is a product of the Reformation era, and although it is now more than 400 years old, remains a most valuable tool for study. Along with the KJV we are pleased to present the English Standard Version, which has rapidly become one of the most widely used modern English translations. The success of the ESV is due in part to the translators' efforts to follow sound, classical principals of translation very like those used by the KJV translators. The result is a very readable English translation that also allows readers to grasp the biblical expressions and terms that appear repeatedly in the Bible. Due to this approach, we find the ESV an especially helpful translation for Bible study. Our notes are keyed to the ESV, but we have placed the KJV in parallel with the ESV for easy comparison. Since the ESV text is based on the broad consensus of biblical scholars who have consulted the early Greek manuscripts, it differs at points from the KJV text, which was produced when fewer manuscripts were available for study. Where significant differences between the translations appear, the notes include comment.

Our Prayer for You

The following prayer embodies the sense of study and devotion we wish to convey to all who take up these commentaries:

> Blessed Lord, You have caused all Holy Scriptures to be written for our learning. Grant that we may so hear them, read, mark, learn, and inwardly digest them that, by patience and comfort from Your holy Word, we may embrace and ever hold fast the blessed hope of everlasting life; through Jesus Christ, our Lord. Amen.

Rev. Edward A. Engelbrecht, STM
Senior Editor for Professional and Academic Books
and Bible Resources

ACKNOWLEDGEMENTS

We are grateful to the Lord for the kind service of our editorial assistant, Sarah Steiner, who managed assignments, entered changes, and acquired needed resources. Also noteworthy are the design and typography of our colleagues Jennifer Horton-Beck and Ruth Brown, who gave this first volume of the series a beautiful and easy reading appearance. These are just a few of the many colleages at CPH who make this series possible.

We are also personally grateful for the willing spirit of Rev. Dr. Steven P. Mueller, Professor of Theology and Dean of Christ College at Concordia University—Irvine, CA. Dr. Mueller has agreed to serve as general editor for other volumes in the series. We look forward to his valuable service.

ABBREVIATIONS

AD	*anno Domini* (in the year of [our] Lord)		NT	New Testament
			OT	Old Testament
BC	before Christ		p.	page
c.	circa		pp.	pages
cf.	confer		St.	Saint
ch.	chapter		v.	verse
chs.	chapters		vv.	verses
Gk	Greek			

Scripture

Gn	Genesis		Jnh	Jonah
Ex	Exodus		Mi	Micah
Lv	Leviticus		Na	Nahum
Nu	Numbers		Hab	Habakkuk
Dt	Deuteronomy		Zep	Zephaniah
Jsh	Joshua		Hg	Haggai
Jgs	Judges		Zec	Zechariah
Ru	Ruth		Mal	Malachi
1Sm	1 Samuel			
2Sm	2 Samuel		Mt	Matthew
1Ki	1 Kings		Mk	Mark
2Ki	2 Kings		Lk	Luke
1Ch	1 Chronicles		Jn	John
2Ch	2 Chronicles		Ac	Acts
Ezr	Ezra		Rm	Romans
Ne	Nehemiah		1Co	1 Corinthians
Est	Esther		2Co	2 Corinthians
Jb	Job		Gal	Galatians
Ps	Psalms		Eph	Ephesians
Pr	Proverbs		Php	Philippians
Ec	Ecclesiastes		Col	Colossians
Sg	Song of Solomon		1Th	1 Thessalonians
Is	Isaiah		2Th	2 Thessalonians
Jer	Jeremiah		1Tm	1 Timothy
Lm	Lamentations		2Tm	2 Timothy
Ezk	Ezekiel		Ti	Titus
Dn	Daniel		Phm	Philemon
Hos	Hosea		Heb	Hebrews
Jl	Joel		Jas	James
Am	Amos		1Pt	1 Peter
Ob	Obadiah		2Pt	2 Peter

1Jn	1 John	Jude	Jude
2Jn	2 John	Rv	Revelation
3Jn	3 John		

The Apocrypha

Jth	Judith	Old Grk Est	Old Greek Esther
Wis	The Wisdom of Solomon	Sus	Susanna
Tob	Tobit	Bel	Bel and the Dragon
Ecclus	Ecclesiasticus (aka Sirach)	Pr Az	Prayer of Azariah
Bar	Baruch	Sg Three	The Song of the Three
Lt Jer	The Letter of Jeremiah		Holy Children
1Macc	1 Maccabees	Pr Man	Prayer of Manasseh
2Macc	2 Maccabees		

Other Books

1Esd	1 Esdras	Ps 151	Psalm 151
2Esd	2 Esdras	1En	1 Enoch
3Macc	3 Maccabees	2En	2 Enoch
4Macc	4 Maccabees	Jub	Jubilees

Abbreviations for Commonly Cited Books and Works

AC — Augsburg Confession. From *Concordia*.

ANF — Roberts, Alexander, and James Donaldson, eds. *The Ante-Nicene Fathers: The Writings of the Fathers Down to AD 325*, 10 vols. Buffalo: The Christian Literature Publishing Company, 1885–96. Reprint, Grand Rapids, MI: Eerdmans, 2001.

Ap — Apology of the Augsburg Confession. From *Concordia*.

Bengel — Bengel, John Albert. *Gnomon of the New Testament*. 5 vols. Edinburgh: T. & T. Clark, 1877.

Calvin — Calvin, John. *Commentaries on the Epistles of Paul the Apostle to the Philippians, Colossians, and Thessalonians*. John Pringle, trans. Edinburgh: Calvin Translation Society, 1851.

Chemnitz — Chemnitz, Martin. *Chemnitz's Works*. 8 vols. St. Louis: Concordia, 1971–89.

Church — Huss, John. *The Church*. David S. Schaff, trans. New York: Charles Scribner's Sons, 1915.

Concordia — McCain, Paul Timothy, ed. *Concordia: The Lutheran Confessions*. 2nd ed. St. Louis: Concordia, 2006.

Ep — Epitome of the Formula of Concord. From *Concordia*.

ESV — English Standard Version.

FC — Formula of Concord. From *Concordia*.

Gerhard — Gerhard, Johann. *Theological Commonplaces*. Richard J. Dinda, trans. Benjamin T. G. Mayes, ed. St. Louis: Concordia, 2009–.

H82	*The Hymnal 1982, according to the Use of The Episcopal Church.* New York: The Church Hymnal Corporation, 1985.
KJV	King James Version.
Knox	Knox, John. *Writings of the Rev. John Knox.* London: The Religious Tract Society, 1900.
LC	Large Catechism of Martin Luther. From *Concordia.*
LSB	Commission on Worship of The Lutheran Church—Missouri Synod. *Lutheran Service Book.* St. Louis: Concordia, 2006.
LW	Luther, Martin. *Luther's Works.* American Edition. General editors Jaroslav Pelikan and Helmut T. Lehmann. 56 vols. St. Louis: Concordia, and Philadelphia: Muhlenberg and Fortress, 1955–1986. Vols. 56–75: Edited by Christopher Boyd Brown. St. Louis: Concordia, 2009–.
LXX	Septuagint. Koine Greek Old Testament.
NPNF1	Schaff, Philip, ed. *A Select Library of Nicene and Post-Nicene Fathers of the Christian Church.* Series 1, 14 vols. New York: The Christian Literature Series, 1886–89. Reprint, Grand Rapids, MI: Eerdmans, 1956.
NPNF2	Schaff, Philip, and Henry Wace, ed. *A Select Library of Nicene and Post-Nicene Fathers of the Christian Church,* Series 2, 14 vols. New York: The Christian Literature Series, 1890–99. Reprint, Grand Rapids, MI: Eerdmans, 1952, 1961.
SA	Smalcald Articles. From *Concordia.*
Schaff	Schaff, Philip, ed. *The Creeds of Christendom with a History and Critical Notes.* 3 vols. 4th ed. New York: Harper, 1919.
SD	Solid Declaration of the Formula of Concord. From *Concordia.*
SLSB	Eales, Samuel J., trans. and ed. *Some Letters of St. Bernard, Abbot of Clairvaux.* The Complete Works of S. Bernard, Abbot of Clairvaux 1. London: John Hodges, 1904.
TLWA	Engelbrecht, Edward, comp. and ed. *The Lord Will Answer: A Daily Prayer Catechism Drawn from Holy Scripture, the Church Fathers, and Luther's Small Catechism with Explanation.* St. Louis: Concordia, 2004.
TPH	*The Presbyterian Hymnal.* Louisville, KY: Westminster/John Knox Press, 1990.
Tr	Treatise on the Power and Primacy of the Pope. From *Concordia.*
TUMH	*The United Methodist Hymnal.* Nashville, TN: The United Methodist Publishing House, 1989.
Wesley	Wesley, John. *Explanatory Notes upon the New Testament.* 12th ed. New York: Carlton & Porter, 1754.

TIMELINE FOR PAUL'S LETTERS

Anatolia, Greece, and Rome	Egypt and Africa	Dates	Syria, Canaan, and Israel	Mesopotamia and Persia
		3 BC	The annunciation (inter Apr 17–May 16; Lk 1:26–38); John the Baptist born (Aug; Lk 1:57–66)	
		2 BC	Jesus born (mid Jan to early Feb; Mt 1:25; Lk 2:1–7); Magi visit; flight to Egypt (mid to late in the year; Mt 2)	
		1 BC	Death of Herod the Great (after Jan 10; Mt 2:19); return to Nazareth (Mt 2:19–23)	
		AD 6	Judas the Galilean leads revolt against Rome; Judea, Samaria, and Idumaea combined to form the Roman province of Judea	
		c. 10	Rabbi Hillel dies	
		11	Jesus in temple before the elders (c Apr 8–22; Lk 2:42)	
Tiberius, Roman emperor		14–37		
Revolt in Gaul; grain shortages cause unrest in Rome		21		
		29	Baptism of Jesus (Fall; Lk 3:1–2)	
		30	Jesus at Passover (c Apr 8; Jn 2:20)	
		32	Jesus at Passover (c Apr 15; Jn 6:4); Jesus arrives at Feast of Booths (c Oct 14; Jn 7:14); Feast of Booths (Oct 17 or 18; Jn 7:37)	
Roman senators unable to pay debts; subsidized by Emperor Tiberius		33	Triumphal entry (Sun, Mar 29); Last Supper (Thurs eve, Apr 2); crucifixion (Fri, Apr 3); resurrection (Sun, Apr 5); ascension (May 14; Lk 24:51; Ac 1:9); Pentecost (May 24)	
		36	Paul's conversion (Ac 9:1–31)	
Caligula (Gaius), Roman emperor		37–41	Josephus, Jewish historian, born	

Anatolia, Greece, and Rome	Egypt and Africa	Dates	Syria, Canaan, and Israel	Mesopotamia and Persia
	Philo of Alexandria leads Jewish delegation to Rome	c. 39	Caligula attempts to place statue of himself in Jerusalem temple	
		41	Martyrdom of James (late Mar; Ac 12:2); Peter in prison (Apr; Ac 12:3–4); Passover (May 4; Ac 12:4); Peter leaves Jerusalem (May; Gal 2:11)	
		41–44	Herod Agrippa I rules Judea	
Claudius, Roman emperor		41–54		
Peter on mission in Asia Minor (Spr/Sum; 1Pt 1:1–2); [in Corinth (Fall); at Rome (mid Nov)]		42	Peter in Antioch (May 41– Apr 42; Gal 2:11)	
		44	Herod Agrippa at festival in Caesarea (Mar 5; Ac 12:19); death of Herod Agrippa (Mar 10; Ac 12:21–23)	
		47–48	Paul's 1st missionary journey (Ac 13:1–14:28)	
Paul goes to Macedonia; Barnabas and John Mark go to Cyprus (mid May; Ac 15:36–16:10)		49	Conference in Jerusalem (Ac 15:1–35); Peter goes to Antioch (Feb; Gal 2:11); Paul confronts Peter (Apr; Gal 2:11)	
Paul's 2nd missionary journey (Ac 15:39–18:22)		49–51		
		49–56	[Peter in Antioch (seven years)]	
Paul's 3rd missionary journey (Ac 18:23–21:17)		52–55		
Nero, Roman emperor		54–68		
		55–57	Paul imprisoned in Caesarea (Ac 23:23–26:32)	
Paul's journey to Rome (Ac 27:1–28:16)		57–58		

Anatolia, Greece, and Rome	Egypt and Africa	Dates	Syria, Canaan, and Israel	Mesopotamia and Persia
Paul in custody in Rome (Ac 28:17–31)		58–60		
		62	Martyrdom of James, the Lord's brother	
Paul assigns Titus at Crete (Ti 1:5)		64–65		
Paul in Ephesus, where he leaves Timothy (Spr–Sum; 1Tm 1:3)		65		
		66–70	Jewish revolt against Romans	
Peter and Paul martyred		68		
Emperor Vespasian		69–79		
		70	Titus destroys Jerusalem temple; Rabbon Yohanan ben Zakkai at Yavneh Academy	
		c. 73	Fall of Masada	
Emperor Titus		79–81		
Emperor Domitian		81–96		
		c. 90–115	Rabbon Gamaliel II at Yavneh Academy	
Jews revolt in Cyprus	Jews revolt in Egypt and Cyrene	115–17		Jews revolt in Mesopotamia
		132–35	Bar Kokhba revolt; death of Rabbi Akiva, Yavneh Academy leader who hailed Bar Kokhba as the messiah	

Paul's Missionary Journeys

Paul's First Journey
Paul's Second Journey
Paul's Third Journey

© CONCORDIA PUBLISHING HOUSE

0 ————— 250 MI.

0 ————— 500 KM.

PAUL'S MISSIONARY JOURNEYS (ACTS 13–21)

First journey (AD 47–48): The Holy Spirit sent Saul, Barnabas, and John Mark from Antioch in Syria via Seleucia to Salamis, then overland to Paphos (Ac 13:1–12). The three continued to Perga, where John Mark left them for Jerusalem (13:13). Saul, also called Paul (13:9), and Barnabas continued to Antioch in Pisidia (13:14–50), Iconium (13:51–14:6a), Lystra, and Derbe (14:6b–20), from whence they retraced their steps back to Pisidian Antioch, then went to Attalia and Syrian Antioch (14:21–28).

Second journey (AD 49–51): Paul and Barnabas separated (15:36–39) while in Syrian Antioch. Paul and Silas went through Syria and Cilicia (15:40–41). They came to Derbe and Lystra, where Timothy joined them (16:1–5). The Spirit led them throughout Galatia and Phrygia to Troas, where they continued, via the island of Samothrace (not shown) to Macedonia; then they traveled to Heapolis and Philippi (16:6–40). They continued via Amphipolis and Apollonia to Thessalonica, Berea, Athens, and Corinth (17:1–18:17). Paul stayed 18 months there (18:11). He journeyed via Cenchreae and Ephesus to Caesarea Maritima, Jerusalem and Syrian Antioch (18:18–22).

Third journey (AD 52–55): Paul took the inland route from Syrian Antioch and eventually arrived in Ephesus, where he stayed for two years and three months (18:23–19.41). He visited Macedonia and Achaia, and then sailed from Philippi to Troas (19:21; 20:1–12) on his way to Jerusalem. From Troas, he sailed via Assos, Mitylene, Miletus (where he met the Ephesian elders), Rhodes, and Patara to Tyre (20:13–21:6). He sailed to Ptolemais and Caesarea Maritima, and went on foot from there to Jerusalem (21:7–17).

Colossae and Asia Minor

© CONCORDIA PUBLISHING HOUSE

EARLY CHURCHES IN ASIA MINOR

Colossae was the location of one of the earliest Christian churches in Asia Minor. Other churches in the region were described in the Book of Revelation later in the first century. These locations (marked with squares) included the following: *Ephesus* was an important stop on Paul's second and third missionary journeys (Ac 18:19–21; 19). It successfully vied with *Smyrna* and Pergamum to be the chief city of Asia Minor. Like Smyrna and the other cities mentioned by John, Ephesus embraced the emperor cult. It also held the temple of Artemis. Pergamum boasted of a great library and many pagan temples. *Thyatira* was known for its cloth dyers (Ac 16:14) and for general worldliness. *Sardis* lived to recall its past glory. *Philadelphia* was known for its pagan temples. *Laodicea*, located at an important trade-route junction, was a wool producer and a center of medicine (cf. Col 4:13–16).

COLOSSIANS

INTRODUCTION TO
COLOSSIANS

Overview

Author

Paul the apostle

Date

c. AD 60

Places

Colossae; Laodicea; Hierapolis

People

Paul; Timothy; Colossians; Laodiceans; Tychicus; Onesimus; Aristarchus; Mark; Barnabas; Jesus called Justus; Epaphras; Luke; Demas; Nympha; Archippus

Purpose

To guide the Colossian congregation away from heresy and into the truth about Jesus and His saving work

Law and Sin Themes

Threat of false teaching and self-made religion; Satan's domain; struggle to fulfill God's calling; God's coming wrath; the old self; admonish one another; God's order for families and labor

Grace and Gospel Themes

Gospel growth; the Son's kingdom and reign; mystery: Christ dwells in you; Baptism, the new circumcision; the new self; the Lord's inheritance

Memory Verses

Transferred to God's kingdom (1:11–14); hymn of Christ (1:15–20); the new circumcision (2:11–14); shadow and substance (2:16–17); glory above (3:1–4)

Luther on Colossians

Just as the Epistle to the Galatians resembles and is modeled on the Epistle to the Romans, comprising in outline the same material that is more fully and richly developed in Romans; so this epistle resembles that to the Ephesians and comprises also in outline the same contents.

First [Paul] praises and wishes for the Colossians, that they continue and increase in faith. He delineates what the gospel and faith are, namely, a wisdom which recognizes Christ as Lord and God, crucified for us, which has been hidden for ages but now brought into the open through his ministry. This is the first chapter.

In chapter 2 he warns them against the doctrines of men, which are always contrary to faith. He depicts these doctrines more clearly than they are depicted anywhere else in Scripture, and criticizes them in a masterly way.

In chapter 3 he exhorts them to be fruitful in the pure faith, doing all sorts of good works for one another, and he describes for some various stations in life the works which are appropriate to them.

In chapter 4 he commends himself to their prayers and gives them greetings and encouragement. (LW 35:386)

Calvin on the Colossian Heresy

In the first place, it is abundantly evident, from Paul's words, that those profligates were intent upon this—that they might mix up Christ with Moses, and might retain the shadows of the law along with the gospel. Hence it is probable that they were Jews. As, however, they coloured over their fallacies with specious disguises, Paul, on this account, calls it a vain philosophy. (Colossians 2:8) At the same time, in employing that term, he had in his eye, in my opinion, the speculations with which they amused themselves, which were subtle, it is true, but at the same time useless and profane: for they contrived a way of access to God through means of angels, and put forth many speculations of that nature, such as are contained in the books of Dionysius on the Celestial Hierarchy, drawn from the school of the Platonists. This, therefore, is the principal object at which he aims—to teach that all things are in Christ, and that he alone ought to be reckoned amply sufficient by the Colossians. (Calvin 133–34)

Gerhard on Colossians

Colosse was the principal city of Phrygia in Asia Minor, near Laodicea. There Epaphras, a fellow worker of the apostles, had gathered a congregation by preaching the Gospel. The apostle directed this Epistle to the inhabitants of that city. Although the people of Rhodes are found to have been called "Colossians" [Colossenses] because of their famous Colossus, the apostle nevertheless addresses not them but the residents of Phrygia. The occasion for its writing was this: The Colossians had been attacked by false teachers. Some of these, who had come from Judaism, were confusing Moses with Christ and were arguing that the ceremonies of the Law were necessary for salvation. Some, who had been converted to the Christian faith from heathenism, were urging human rules from the teachings of philosophers. At Epaphrus's request, therefore, Paul wrote this Epistle to them from his captivity in Rome to strengthen them in the true faith and safeguard them against the false teachers. (Gerhard E 1.263)

Challenges for Readers

Authorship and Date. Though the early Christians uniformly believed that Paul wrote this Letter, critics have assumed that a disciple of Paul wrote it. The critics see significant differences from Paul's other Letters in the style of the sentences, some unique terms and expressions, and the Letter's general character, though all agree that this Letter bears great similarity to Ephesians. Critics commonly date Colossians to the last generation of the first century rather than the traditional dating to the middle of the first century. In this commentary we work with the traditional dating and attribute the Letter to the apostle Paul since the arguments of the critics do not take into account fully Paul's habit of writing his Letters with the help of scribes, who would affect the style of writing (cf. Rm 16:22; Gal 6:11).

Firstborn. The early heretic Arius (c. AD 260–336) and modern groups such as the Jehovah's Witnesses have sadly misunderstood Paul's words in Col 1:15, suggesting that Jesus is a created being and not true, eternal God. But Paul used the expression "firstborn of all creation" not to describe Christ as a creature but to describe His right as a firstborn: He is ruler and heir of all creation, for He existed before creation and all things were created through Him and for Him (1:16–17).

Gnosticism and the Colossian Heresy. Our knowledge of the heresy combated by the letter to the Colossians is limited to those passages in the letter in which the apostle writes against it. Paul's references to Jewish practices (2:11), festivals (2:16), and dietary scruples (2:20) point to a Jewish element to the Colossian heresy. Nevertheless, the false teaching against which this letter was written differed from the simple Judaizing countered by the apostle's letters to the Philippians and especially to the Galatians. In opposing the heresy at Colossae, Paul laid great stress on the correct teaching concerning the person and work of Christ. He gave emphasis to terms and concepts such as fullness . . . and filling (1:19; 2:9–10), knowledge (2:3), wisdom and understanding (1:6, 9–10, 27, 28; 2:2–3, 23; 3:10),

5

the revelation of mysteries (1:26–27; 2:2), the flesh (1:22, 24; 2:1, 5, 11, 13, 18, 23; 3:22), and perfection (1:28; cf. 3:14; 4:12). He spoke against a religious practice that was exclusive (1:28), had great interest in cosmic beings (1:16; 2:8, 10, 15, 18, 20), and valued its initiations (2:18) and asceticism (2:20–23). From this we see that the Colossian heresy bore a number of similarities to the Gnosticism of the second and third centuries AD. This suggests that like several other NT documents, the letter to the Colossians was written against a point of view which later developed to become (at least an element of) the religious movement known as Gnosticism. (From Paul E. Deterding, *Colossians*. Concordia Commentary. [St. Louis: Concordia, 2003] 7–8.)

Blessings for Readers

The new movement at Colossae meant evil, for it was an attack, all the more vicious because it was not a frontal attack, upon the fact that dominates the whole New Testament, the sole Lordship of the Lord Jesus Christ. But God meant it for good; He gave us in Paul's Letter to the Colossians a proclamation of the Lord Jesus Christ in unparalleled fullness and depth.

The Letter to the Colossians is also a striking fulfillment of the promise of Jesus to His disciples, "Every scribe who has been trained for the kingdom of heaven is like a householder who brings out of his treasure what is new and what is old" (Mt 13:52). The apostles of Jesus are not merely disciples of a great teacher, whose sacred duty it is to pass on their master's words unchanged. They are witnesses to Him who has all authority in heaven and on earth, and they have the Spirit as His gift, the Spirit who leads them into all truth and thus glorifies the Christ. At the time of the church's need, the Spirit opened up to Paul dimensions of the glory of the Christ which the new people of God had not apprehended so fully before.

Though Colossians is one of Paul's shorter Letters, it is especially rich with descriptions of Christ, His work, and the blessings He extends to us through Holy Baptism. As you study Colossians, pray that the Lord would protect your congregation and all Christians from false teachers, for in Christ alone "we have redemption, the forgiveness of sins" (1:14).

Outline

I. Preaching (chs. 1–2)
   A. Salutation (1:1–2)
   B. Overture (1:3–20)
      1. Thanksgiving report (1:3–8)
      2. The source of knowledge: reason for intercession (1:9–14)
      3. The Christ hymn: creation and reconciliation (1:15–20)
   C. Main Exposition and Resolution (1:21–2:23)
      1. Ministry of reconciliation (1:21–29)
      2. True knowledge (2:1–5)
      3. The fullness of Christ (2:6–15)
      4. True freedom (2:16–23)

II. Paul's Instructions (chs. 3–4)
   A. The Christian Life (3:1–4:6)
      1. Death and life (3:1–4)
      2. Put off and put on (3:5–17)
      3. Table of duties (3:18–4:1)
      4. Watch and pray (4:2–6)
   B. Concluding Matters (4:7–18)

PART 1

PREACHING (CHS. 1–2)

Salutation (1:1–2)

ESV	KJV
1 ¹Paul, an apostle of Christ Jesus by the will of God, and Timothy our brother, ²To the saints and faithful brothers in Christ at Colossae: Grace to you and peace from God our Father.	1 ¹Paul, an apostle of Jesus Christ by the will of God, and Timotheus our brother, ²To the saints and faithful brethren in Christ which are at Colosse: Grace be unto you, and peace, from God our Father and the Lord Jesus Christ.

Introduction to 1:1–2 The apostle Paul was one of the great letter writers of the Early Church. He maintained contact with the congregations under his care and influenced others through his many letters. In this case, Paul wrote to a church that was founded under his guidance by one of his faithful coworkers, Timothy, whom we know from the Book of Acts 16:1–5 and from Paul's Letters to Timothy. The Letter to the Colossians shows that the situation there was unusual. In other letters Paul dealt with disputes among members who had different ideas about how things should be done. However, this young church at Colossae was threatened by something far more dangerous: false belief that directed people away from Christ and His work and pointed the people toward themselves. The apostle wrote to the Colossian Christians to restore them to the truths they were taught and thereby strengthen them to resist the challenges to their faith that they were facing.

Letters in the Greco-Roman world followed a standard pattern. We see this pattern at work in Paul's Letter to the Colossians. For example, if Julius wrote to Apollo, he would begin his letter "Julius to Apollo, greetings." The apostle Paul's Letters follow a modified form of this greeting. Sometimes Paul added further thoughts to the basic style. In the present Letter he wrote, "Paul . . . to the . . . brothers . . . at Colossae: Grace . . ." (in Greek the words for "greetings" and "grace" are even more similar than their English equivalents are). To his salutation of "grace" the apostle also added the common Semitic or Jewish greeting, "peace" (cf. Dn 4:1). How significant it is that Paul's Letter begins where the Christian life begins—where the Colossians had begun—in the grace of the Lord Jesus Christ!

1:1 *apostle.* This word comes from the Greek *apostolos,* meaning "sent one." It describes a person acting under authority and on behalf of another—a man on a mission. When this word is used in its technical Christian sense (as here), it describes one sent with the full authority of God or Christ. (On the authority of Paul's writings, see also the note at 4:16. See further the comments on "tradition" in the note at 2Th 2:15.) So, when Paul writes as an apostle, his words are God's own words. Paul identified himself as an apostle in all of his Letters except Php, 2Th, and Phm; he thereby established his authority as one appointed directly by the risen Lord, whom he had seen (1Co 9:2; 15:8). *by the will of God.* Does a faithful servant choose to send himself on a mission? By pointing to the "will of God," Paul showed that it was not his idea to "turn the world upside down" (Ac 17:6). God made him an apostle, investing His authority in Paul for the sake of the mission. *Timothy.* Paul's younger co-worker in the Gospel was the son of a Gentile father and a Jewish mother (Ac 16:1). Intermarriage between persons of different cultures was common outside of Israel, though not without complications, just as one finds for families today. Timothy often worked alongside Paul (e.g., Php 2:22). He must have been a diligent young man, for he gained Paul's trust. Paul sent Timothy as his representative on various occasions (e.g., 1Co 4:17; 1Th 3:2). Today that sounds glorious—representing the great apostle! But at that time, when the Church was small, it was probably a very humble task for a small but growing circle of people. The use of the plural (e.g., "we") in vv. 3–4, 9, and 28 shows that at least in a limited sense Paul considered Timothy a contributor to this letter.

1:2 *saints.* This word has a rich background in the OT where it was used often in the Psalms (e.g., Ps 132:9, 16). It may be translated "holy ones" and refers to God's people generally, not to greater or more noble persons. Christians are made holy through faith or trust in Christ, through whom they receive the forgiveness of all their un-holiness. Christ takes our sin and gives us His holiness, sending to us His Holy Spirit (Lk 11:13). *faithful brothers.* Paul, like other Jewish writers, liked to use family terms when describing relationships. The "brothers" are fellow believers (Rm 8:29). This title is sometimes used of fellow laborers in Christ's mission (1Co 16:11–12; 2Co 8:23), perhaps in contrast to typical members of a congregation. *in Christ.* By Baptism and the Word of God, we are brought to saving faith; through such faith we are "in Christ." This prepositional phrase denotes a unique relationship that believers have with Christ—they are connected to Him or belong to Him in a favorable (saving) relationship (2:11–13; Rm 6:3, 11; Gal 3:26–27; Eph 1:13; 3:6). *Colossae.* The city where Paul's readers dwelt was in the Roman province of Asia (modern Turkey), about 100 mi E of Ephesus. It stood on the banks of the Lycus River with rugged mountains nearby, a stop along the busy trade route between the Greek world and the east. Based on later portions of the Letter, Epaphras most likely brought the Gospel to Colossae as well as to Laodicea and Hierapolis (see the notes at 1:6, 7; 4:12, 13).

1:1–2 in Devotion and Prayer False teachings were tempting the Colossian Christians to give up on the faith they had been taught. A great spiritual battlefield was forming between truth and error, good and evil, death and life. But God would not abandon the little gathering of believers in Colossae. He sent Paul, Timothy, and other faithful servants to establish the truth and love of Christ in their hearts. We too face false teachings that would rend us away from Christ, sever our congregations, and divide our families. But God does not give up on us either. Through the Holy Scriptures, and those who faithfully proclaim and teach these to us, He calls us His saints. The Lord draws us shoulder to shoulder as faithful brothers so that we strengthen one another and remain faithful to Him. How faithful He is to us! • O Lord, send from heaven and save me; put to shame him who tramples on me. Send out Your steadfast love and Your faithfulness! Amen. (paraphrase of Ps 57:4)

Overture (1:3–20)

Thanksgiving report (1:3–8)

ESV	KJV
[3]We always thank God, the Father of our Lord Jesus Christ, when we pray for you, [4]since we heard of your faith in Christ Jesus and of the love that you have for all the saints, [5]because of the hope laid up for you in heaven. Of this you have heard before in the word of the truth, the gospel, [6]which has come to you, as indeed in the whole world it is bearing fruit and growing—as it also does among you, since the day you heard it and understood the grace of God in truth, [7]just as you learned it from Epaphras our beloved fellow servant. He is a faithful minister of Christ on your behalf [8]and has made known to us your love in the Spirit.	[3]We give thanks to God and the Father of our Lord Jesus Christ, praying always for you, [4]Since we heard of your faith in Christ Jesus, and of the love which ye have to all the saints, [5]For the hope which is laid up for you in heaven, whereof ye heard before in the word of the truth of the gospel; [6]Which is come unto you, as it is in all the world; and bringeth forth fruit, as it doth also in you, since the day ye heard of it, and knew the grace of God in truth: [7]As ye also learned of Epaphras our dear fellow servant, who is for you a faithful minister of Christ; [8]Who also declared unto us your love in the Spirit.

Introduction to 1:3–14 As the overture of a symphony introduces musical themes that will be prominent in the rest of the symphony, so with Col 1:3–20 Paul premiered themes that he would develop more fully in the remainder of this Letter. Among the more significant of these themes are hope (1:5, 23, 27), the Word/Gospel of God (1:5, 23, 25, 3:16; 4:5), knowledge (1:9, 10; 2:2, 3; 3:10), servants/ministers of God's Word (1:7, 23, 25; 4:7, 12, 17), filled/fullness (1:9, 19; 2:9-10), wisdom (1:9, 28; 2:2, 23; 3:16; 4:5), "authorities" (1:13, 16; 2:8, 10, 15, 18, 20), forgiveness (1:14; 2:13), Christ's full deity (1:15, 19; 2:9), image of God (1:15; 3:10), Christ as head of His body, the Church (1:18, 24; 2:19; 3:15), Christ's resurrection (1:18); 2:12), reconciliation (1:20, 22), and Christ's death (1:20, 22; 2:14, 20).

This "Overture" may be divided into 3 parts: (1) a report of those things about the Colossians that move the apostle to give thanks to

God (1:3–8), (2) a section on the true wisdom and knowledge that the apostle prayed his readers would have (1:9–14), and (3) a hymn regarding the divine Christ and His work of creation and reconciliation (1:15–20).

Another feature of these verses is the long opening sentence contained in vv. 3–7 (in Greek v. 8 is also part of this sentence). Paul was writing with a bit of flourish, which was typical of Greek style. One often finds these long, more complicated sentences at the beginning of a letter, treatise, or address. It was sort of the Greek way of saying, "Look what I can do! You should listen carefully." Does the apostle have your attention?

1:3 *thank.* This is another common feature of Greek letter writing, patting the readers on the back before getting into the body of the letter. (See the introduction to 2Th 1:3–4.) Paul would have some hard words to share with the Colossians but he wanted them to know that he thought of them often and with prayerful intent. *the Father of our Lord Jesus Christ.* Paul had already described God as the Father of the Christians at Colossae (v. 2). But now he emphasized another relationship that is important to the Father, indeed, the most important of all. God is first of all the Father of His Son, our Savior Jesus, whose relationship to the Father was questioned by the Colossian false teachers. In conjunction with 1:8 ("Spirit"), Paul pointed to God's triune nature and made the message of the entire Letter explicitly Trinitarian. Knowing the God we address, calling on Him rightly in prayer, is essential for a truth faith and genuine worship that honors the one true God. *Lord.* The Greek word is *kyrios*, which is used thousands of times in the Greek translation of the OT, the Septuagint (LXX). It translates God's personal Hebrew name, Yahweh. Note that the NT regularly applies *kyrios* to Jesus to identify Him with the OT name Yahweh and hence to designate Jesus as true God (1Co 12:3; Php 2:9). *when we pray for you.* Fervent prayer is an important part of Christian ministry (cf. 1:9; 4:2–3, 12). Based on these words, it appears that Paul prayed frequently for the Colossians, though he did not tell us how often.

1:4 *heard.* Apart from a few individuals, Paul had not met the Colossians face-to-face (cf. 2:1). They were subject to his care through Timothy, as described in the notes on v. 1.

1:5 *hope laid up.* Most people in the Greco-Roman world lived without hope (cf. Eph 2:12; see also the note at 1Th 4:13). They followed religions based on fear of the gods and duty to them. Many millions lived as slaves in life-long subjugation without the opportunity to dream of a better future. Hope can be thought of as faith directed toward the future. Here the term designates the content of Christianity, that is "**the** hope" upon which our activity of believing ("faith") rests and out of which our love for others flows ("faith . . . love . . . because of the hope"; vv. 4–5; cf. 1Co 13:13). *gospel.* Paul reminded them about the message of salvation in Christ (cf. 1Co 15:1–4; Rm 1:16) through which they became God's children and brothers to one another. Unlike the false teachers, Paul emphasized the reliability of the saving work and word of Christ as revealed in the Gospel, the "good news" that inspires hope for this life and reserves for us a home in the life to come.

1:6 *come to you.* As the founding missionary of the Colossian Church, Epaphras had brought the Gospel to them (v. 7). Paul wrote as though the Gospel was a living, breathing person who walked into their lives—and it is! Epaphras did not preach some empty words but the words that present Christ and make known the Spirit. God's Word is lively and life giving. *in the whole world.* In a mere three decades since Pentecost, Jesus' disciples proclaimed the Gospel from the sunrise border of the Roman Empire in Syria to the sunset beaches in Spain. Disciples raced through the entire Roman world (see 1:23 and note; see also 1Tm 3:16), taking fullest advantage of the empire's advanced transportation network on land and sea. Note also that the narrative of the Book of Acts ends with Paul's unhindered speaking of the Gospel in Rome itself, the heart and nerve of the empire. In this way the Lord fulfilled the promise of Jesus in Ac 1:8 that His followers would be His witnesses "to the end of the earth." Would that He might loose our feet and mouths to do the same today. *bearing fruit and growing.* The Gospel (v. 5) produces faith and good works and causes believers to grow in these blessings of the Christian life; cf. Gal 5:22–23. Paul's description includes the fruit of new believers added to the congregation through the example and testimony of those who boldly confess their Lord. *grace.* As noted above (v. 2), this is a word of major importance in the Scriptures and one that every Christian should cleanly grasp. It describes the generous favor of God toward undeserving people (Rm 5:12–21; Ti 3:3–7). This is not favor as in our expression, "Can you do me a favor?" It is no mere random act of kindness. Paul described the lavish love and favor God shows toward those He gathers to be His children. The heavenly Father loves His children, favors, and treasures them with blessings, though they cannot repay Him one bit. Set in your mind the picture of new parents adoring their helpless newborn, and you glimpse the favor Paul envisioned. See again a father running to receive his lost son (Lk 15:20–24), and you catch another view of this favor that is ours through the Gospel. See also the note at 4:18.

1:7 *Epaphras.* Paul was very close to this brother and called him a "fellow prisoner" in Phm 23. Above we noted what an honor it might seem to represent the great apostle (v. 1). Here we see the truth of it: chains awaited Paul's companions. Although the Gospel inspired hope in believers, it inspired fear in others who could not understand and believe its message. But Colossae was Epaphras's little part of the empire where God would bring forth through him the "fruit" and "growth" of the Gospel (v. 6). Epaphras was likely the first one to scratch and sow in this field of the kingdom, as these verses hint. *on your behalf.* Many manuscripts have "on our behalf," a reading many scholars prefer, which would indicate that Epaphras diligently served or shared the purposes of Paul and Timothy. Indeed, "our" shows that Epaphras carried out his ministry on Paul's behalf and under his oversight. *minister.* This renders the Greek word *diakonos*, a general term for a servant (Jn 2:5), but in the NT it is often used of one who serves/ministers with the Gospel (2Co 3:6; Eph 3:7; Col 1:23, 25). In fact, "deacon" became the title for a church worker in those early days, though we do not know precisely when and cannot always tells whether a formal office of service was intended. Special offices were anticipated by servants in the OT. Many OT believers were called slaves (servants) of God: Moses (Ps 105:26), Joshua (Jsh 24:29), David (2Sm 7:5), and Jeremiah (Jer 7:25).

1:8 *love in the Spirit.* Love as well as faith is the work of the Holy Spirit through the Gospel, who stirs us to hope for blessings yet unseen. So ends Paul's first theme in the overture of thanks and prayer for the Colossians.

The source of knowledge: reason for intercession (1:9–14)

ESV	KJV
[9]And so, from the day we heard, we have not ceased to pray for you, asking that you may be filled with the knowledge of his will in all spiritual wisdom and understanding, [10]so as to walk in a manner worthy of the Lord, fully pleasing to him, bearing fruit in every good work and increasing in the knowledge of God. [11]May you be strengthened with all power, according to his glorious might, for all endurance and patience with joy, [12]giving thanks to the Father, who has qualified you to share in the inheritance of the saints in light. [13]He has delivered us from the domain of darkness and transferred us to the kingdom of his beloved Son, [14]in whom we have redemption, the forgiveness of sins.	[9]For this cause we also, since the day we heard it, do not cease to pray for you, and to desire that ye might be filled with the knowledge of his will in all wisdom and spiritual understanding; [10]That ye might walk worthy of the Lord unto all pleasing, being fruitful in every good work, and increasing in the knowledge of God; [11]Strengthened with all might, according to his glorious power, unto all patience and longsuffering with joyfulness; [12]Giving thanks unto the Father, which hath made us meet to be partakers of the inheritance of the saints in light: [13]Who hath delivered us from the power of darkness, and hath translated us into the kingdom of his dear Son: [14]In whom we have redemption through his blood, even the forgiveness of sins:

1:9–12 In these verses we see what a man of prayer Paul was and how he encouraged such prayer among his fellow workers and in the congregations. Paul prayed about the entire Christian life: for faith (v. 9), for the living of our faith (v. 10), for strength when we meet resistance (v. 11), and for the final outcome of faith—eternal life (v. 12). The spiritual focus of his prayer is especially noteworthy in a day when we are prone to pray for physical or material needs first and most often. Paul set forth a marked example of the truth that Christians are engaged in spiritual warfare and spiritual life above all other concerns.

1:9 *pray.* Paul's attention to regular prayer was an integral aspect of his ministry. Take a moment to flip through the Bible and look at the first chapter in each of his letters and you will discover how often he began with thanks and prayer. *knowledge*. From Greek *epignosis*. False teachers at Colossae had promoted another kind of knowledge, one that they asserted was hidden from the majority of people and which needed to be made known by those who, like them, had been initiated into the secrets/mysteries of salvation. Some commentators believe that these false teachers taught an early form of Gnosticism, which severely challenged Christianity later in the first century and in the second century AD. (For more on the Colossian heresy, see the introduction.) In contrast to false teaching, Paul prayed here for knowledge that is centered in God's forgiveness in Christ (v. 14) and revealed by the Holy Spirit. *wisdom*. The Greek term is *sophia*. Paul used this word six times in the Letter (1:9, 28; 2:3, 23; 3:16; 4:5), which shows that it was a significant emphasis for him to this congregation. Although similar in meaning to "knowledge" and "understanding," the word "wisdom" emphasizes that faith is a practical ability for godly living in the real world. Our world is functional and sound because God created it with wisdom (Pr 3:19–20) and imparted wisdom to His creation (Jb 28:20, 23–27). Hence, true wisdom is a necessary gift from God the Creator and Redeemer. You need this gift if you are to live in harmony with God's ways and God's world. *understanding*. This is another term for "knowledge" and "wisdom;" the adjective "spiritual" indicates that this understanding is a gift of the Holy Spirit (1:8). Calvin wrote,

> [Paul] intimates that the will of God, of which he had made mention, was the only rule of right knowledge. For if any one is desirous simply to know those things which it has pleased God to reveal, that is the man who accurately knows what it is to be truly wise. If we desire anything beyond that, this will be nothing else than to be foolish, by not keeping within due bounds. . . . So long as men are regulated by their own carnal perceptions, they have also their own wisdom, but it is of such a nature as is mere vanity, however much they may delight themselves in it (Calvin 143).

1:10 *walk*. In both the OT and the NT this word often refers to faith-based ethical conduct (one's "way of life"). Think, for example, of God's call to Abram when He gave him the covenant of circumcision. The Lord began, "I am God Almighty; walk before me, and be blameless" (Gn 17:1). *worthy*. The Greek word here, *axios* ("suitable to") is related to English "axiomatic," "taken for granted." The new

17

life comes from Christ and flows naturally from true faith in Him; it is "axiomatic" that one with true faith in Christ will be empowered and motivated by that faith to begin living the God-pleasing life. Luther wrote,

> Faith, however, is a divine work in us which changes us and makes us to be born anew of God, John 1[:12–13]. It kills the old Adam and makes us altogether different men, in heart and in spirit and mind and powers; and it brings with it the Holy Spirit. O it is a living, busy, active, mighty thing, this faith. It is impossible for it not to be doing good works incessantly (LW 35:370).

bearing fruit. This expression may reflect the teaching of Jesus; see Mt 7:16–20; 13:3–23. This wording and the similar one of 1:6 also indicates that godly living is a natural outgrowth of faith in Christ. Notice how Paul described the Christian life with experiences common to his hearers, who most often walked everywhere they went and who likely passed rows of olive trees, grape vines, and other fruit-bearing plants along the way. If Paul would describe our lives today, he might write about how we drive before the Lord and turn a profit. What we believe and put into practice as believers encompasses not only our quiet strolls through the orchard but perhaps most importantly the daily business of our lives.

1:11 *power.* The Greek term is *dynamis*, from which comes the English word "dynamite." God empowers His people for service. The explosive growth of the Church in the first century is an example of God's power at work through His people. *glorious might.* This phrase denotes dazzling power; it is used only of God in the NT. Since Paul will shortly describe the spiritual warfare (v. 13) that surrounds God's kingdom, his emphasis on the source of our strength bolsters his prayer. *endurance.* Suffering does not erode endurance (2Co 1:6), which holds fast to hope in Christ (Rm 8:25; 15:4). It persists in good works (Rm 2:7) and produces proven character (Rm 5:4). *patience.* "Longsuffering" may be a better rendering, as the true character of patience is seen in its enduring even in the face of trials. Paul joined "endurance" and "patience" with another word we might not expect. His thought might seem ordinary to us if he had said that we are patient and endure bravely. But instead Paul linked these works with joy. Jesus did the same at the conclusion of the Beatitudes when He urged His disciples to rejoice while facing persecution (Mt 5:12). Is Christianity then some sort of sadistic religion, or one that teaches people to simply accept the suffering of life and make little effort to improve our lot? Some have made such charges, describing religion as opium that lulls people into quietness when revolution is needed. They do not understand the revolutionary work of the Gospel!

1:12 *qualified you.* Sin disqualifies us. God overturns its effects and has qualified us through Christ's redemption (v. 14). *inheritance.* Recall the inheritance of the Promised Land that was allotted to the families of Israel according to God's promises and not because of their righteousness (Dt 9:5). This is one of the most beautiful images of the blessings of the Gospel. Just as a child does nothing to be part of the family and to be a partaker in its blessings and wealth, so we do nothing to earn a place in God's family. We simply receive the blessings of the kingdom of God. He declares us worthy (v. 10) even though we totter and fall. The resurrection to eternal life in heaven is the fulfillment of Israel's inheritance of the Promised Land and is also a gift of God's grace rather than something we earn. *saints in light.* See the note on "saints" at 1:2. Although believers were at one time in the darkness of sin and death (e.g., Eph 5:8), through Christ's redemption we are no longer separated from God, who is "light" (Jn 8:12; see further the note on v. 13). Just as the saints in eternity enjoy their inheritance, so we are now qualified for the same. Everlasting life is present now for heirs of the kingdom.

1:13 Paul switched from praying for the Colossian congregation to describing what God has already done for them. He remembered the moment when the tide of spiritual battle turned. *delivered . . . transferred.* The past tense of these verbs points the Colossians back to Baptism, which incorporated them into Christ's saving work (2:6–15). *domain of darkness.* Melanchthon wrote: "Human nature has been delivered into slavery and is held captive by the devil" (Ap II 47). The NT often uses light/darkness for the contrast between God/Satan, salvation/sin (Ac 26:18). The writers of the Dead Sea Scrolls likewise drew on this imagery. Biblical and Jewish usage differs from that of some later Gnostics and Manichaeans, who used this comparison as though God and Satan were equal forces. God's power to save from the darkness of sin applies for all people and overpowers the evil one. His "glorious might" (v. 11) breaches the darkness and envelopes us, just as rescuing soldiers breach prison walls and flood the dark chambers with new light. In that moment the prisoners who could see only darkness are awash in the glorious freedom brought

19

to them. *kingdom*. This word reflects Jesus' extensive teaching on the kingdom of God/heaven. (In the Gospels it is often preferable to translate this term as "reign" or "rule," since it denotes God's gracious action on our behalf rather than a place, which the translation "kingdom" might imply.) This saving "reign" of God began with Christ's own coming (Mt 4:17), which came through the forgiveness of sins (Mt 16:18–19; 18:23–27) that Jesus acquired for us by His death (Mt 21:33–46). It now comes to us personally through God's Word (Mt 13:3–8). In a similar way Paul here wrote of God's kingdom/reign in connection with Christ's forgiveness (v. 14), and in this letter he made many references to the Word of God. Paul's description of salvation in this passage is one of the most dynamic in all of Holy Scripture!

1:14 *redemption*. To redeem is to "buy back" a slave or captive and thus to set him/her free. The KJV includes the words "through His blood," which appear in some Greek manuscripts and early Bible translations. The phrase emphasizes that Christ paid the price for our redemption by His death on the cross (e.g., Gal 3:13). *forgiveness*. The Greek term pictures forgiveness as "letting go" or "dismissing" sin or debt. Paul put redemption and forgiveness together. This may have been in contrast to the idea that forgiveness was only a preliminary step of salvation, a teaching held by some later Gnostics. Salvation is the point and not simply a step on the way to something else. Yet with salvation comes a host of blessings noted by the apostle: knowledge of God's will, strength, endurance, joy, and an everlasting inheritance. Luther noted,

> No one is baptized in order that he may become a prince, but, as the words say, that he 'be saved.' We know that to be saved is nothing other than to be delivered from sin, death, and the devil (LC IV 24–25).

1:3–14 in Devotion and Prayer Paul's prayer shows just how much he cared for these new Christians, and he knew that God cared for them even more. Unfortunately, false teachings compete for the Colossians' attention; they lead people to look to themselves instead of looking to God. In the background, the apostle prays fervently for them so that they would not fall prey again to the darkness from which the Lord has rescued them. In the foreground, Paul boldly proclaims the true wisdom of redemption in Jesus, shining the light of their eternal inheritance in the Gospel.

We have all been tempted to look to other things instead of Jesus for our salvation. But only in Christ is there the divine knowledge and wisdom that will bring eternal good. • Thank You, O God, for Your patience and persistence to save us through Your beloved Son. Fill us now with all joy in Christ as we endure whatever life may send. Amen.

The Image of God

In the beginning, God created man in His own likeness (Genesis 1:26–27). In this consists his dignity, which is not the result of development and behavior, but of God's act. Man is created by God like God, but he himself is not God. However, Exodus 20:4–5 says: "You shall not make for yourself a carved image—any likeness of anything that is in heaven above, or that is in the earth beneath, or that is in the water under the earth; you shall not bow down to them nor serve them."

Thus, man, created by God in the image and likeness of God, shall not make for himself an image of God out of the things created by God. Rather, the relationship between God and man lies in the word of God and in the speaking to God thus made possible (Deuteronomy 4). The word of God rules out making Him visible in artifacts and experiences. . . . The fall of man from God through the violation of His commandment entails man putting himself into God's place to "be like God" (Genesis 3:5) and results in separation from God.

It is testified of God, the Son of God made man, that He is "the image of the invisible God, the firstborn over all creation" (Colossians 1:15; 2 Corinthians 4:4); He is "the brightness of his glory and the express image of His person" (Hebrews 1:3). Here the relation between image and formation comes to a full circle when we not only reencounter the origin of creation in the person of Jesus Christ, in His word and work, but when the salvific will of God is carried out through the renewing gift of the Spirit [Romans 8:29]. . . .

Thus, in the image of Christ what is formed anew and shaped in the Christian through the work of Christ becomes visible. This happens in baptism [Romans 6:3–5]. . . . Our likeness with Christ is accomplished by being "grafted" in him through baptism.

With the image of Christ and the formation of Christians a reality is addressed that cannot be seen when God's word is merely perceived as a text of antiquity; when the sacraments are solely understood as passage rites; and when the communion between God and man is reduced to the purely symbolic. . . . The true care of souls is not only about the limited realm of inwardness, but about the whole human being in soul and body. The biblical understanding of salvation always encompasses body and soul, external and internal health concurrently.

Reinhard Slenczka, "Luther's Care of Souls for Our Times," *Concordia Theological Quarterly 67:1* (January 2003), 56–58.

The Christ hymn: creation and reconciliation (1:15–20)

ESV	KJV
[15]He is the image of the invisible God, the firstborn of all creation. [16]For by him all things were created, in heaven and on earth, visible and invisible, whether thrones or dominions or rulers or authorities—all things were created through him and for him. [17]And he is before all things, and in him all things hold together. [18]And he is the head of the body, the church. He is the beginning, the firstborn from the dead, that in everything he might be preeminent. [19]For in him all the fullness of God was pleased to dwell, [20]and through him to reconcile to himself all things, whether on earth or in heaven, making peace by the blood of his cross.	[15]Who is the image of the invisible God, the firstborn of every creature: [16]For by him were all things created, that are in heaven, and that are in earth, visible and invisible, whether they be thrones, or dominions, or principalities, or powers: all things were created by him, and for him: [17]And he is before all things, and by him all things consist. [18]And he is the head of the body, the church: who is the beginning, the firstborn from the dead; that in all things he might have the preeminence. [19]For it pleased the Father that in him should all fulness dwell; [20]And, having made peace through the blood of his cross, by him to reconcile all things unto himself; by him, I say, whether they be things in earth, or things in heaven.

Introduction to 1:15–20 If you were to write a hymn of praise to Jesus Christ, what would you write? In these verses, Paul completed the "Overture" of the letter that he began in v. 3. As you read Paul's words, keep in mind his experience on the road to Damascus when he personally saw the risen Christ and was shaken by that experience (Ac 9:1–19a). Consider also how quickly this experience changed Paul's views of Christ and his own beliefs and behaviors (Ac 9:19b–22). As you read, say with wonder like Paul's, "Who are You, Lord?" (Ac 9:5) and pay careful attention to Paul's answer and description in Col 1:15–20. Pray that the risen Lord would open the eyes of your heart to see what the world cannot see.

Paul structured these verses with two balanced sections (vv. 15–18a, 18b–20). Each begins with a pronoun referring to Christ, identifies our Lord by the name "firstborn," and includes the phrases "in Him," "through Him," and "for/to/unto Him." In addition we find in each section the phrases "all things," "in the heavens," and "on the earth." This carefully balanced structure and the section's compact, lyrical vocabulary suggest that it is a hymn or is at least based on a hymn. In fact, the editors for the Greek New Testament set these words as lines of poetry. Some scholars believe Paul reworded a hymn used by the proponents of the Colossian heresy. It seems more likely that this section is (or is based on) a hymn used by the Colossians. The similarities of these verses with other portions of Paul's letters strongly suggest that the apostle himself is the author of the hymn. In its two parts the hymn presents Jesus as the agent of creation (vv. 15–18a) and of reconciliation (vv. 18b–20).

1:15 *image.* The Greek word *eikon* describes something that resembles the original, such as the image of Caesar on a coin (Mt 22:20). You will likely recognize our English word "icon" in this Greek word and perhaps think of some of the famous paintings or mosaics of Jesus. Paul wrote that Jesus of Nazareth is the visible image of the invisible God. How does that work? How does one see the unseen? Paul stated a profound paradox and mystery that is beyond mere human comprehension. Often when we suddenly understand something difficult, we say, "I see!" In personal conversations one may even witness blind persons using this common English expression for what happens when the light goes on in your head and you suddenly "get it." But Paul was describing something even more surprising here. While the disciples looked upon Jesus—who looked like any other Jewish man of His day—they realized that in seeing Jesus, they had seen the eternal God (cf. Jn 14:9). Hence, this truth must be revealed to us by God Himself (through His Word) and can only be grasped by faith (Mt 16:16–17). Beginning with this paradox, Paul celebrated both the mystery of God and the mystery of the salvation that is revealed to us in God's Son.

The term "image" also recalls that Adam was created in the image of God (Gn 1:26–28) and points to a contrast between Adam and Christ, the Last Adam (cf. 1Co 15:45). The first Adam sought the following:

(A) he desired to be like God,

(B) he sought to exalt himself,

(C) he disobeyed God, and

(D) thereby he lost the divine image for mankind.

In contrast, Jesus Christ acted differently:

(A) He did not grasp for equality with God,

(B) He humbled Himself,

(C) He was obedient to death on a cross, and

(D) thereby He regained God's image for mankind! (Php 2:5–8; 2Co 3:18; see also AC II 1–2; LC II 65).

firstborn. Paul's opening paradox is challenging. Persons unfamiliar with the biblical context for Paul's expressions have badly misunderstood his next point. For example, Arius (a fourth-century heretic) misunderstood "firstborn" to mean "the first of many creatures," as if Jesus Christ were part of God's creation. Today, Jehovah's Witnesses make similar arguments. However, we know that such an idea is incorrect from other passages of Scripture, which explain that all things were created through Jesus (e.g., Jn 1:1–3). The early Christian bishop, Athanasius (c. 296–373), also pointed out from the immediate context of this passage that this "firstborn" is not a part of the creation but the cause of creation (v. 17; *NPNF*2 4:383). As a result, the KJV translation ("firstborn of every creature") may more clearly indicate that Christ is not a part of the creation but rather the source of everything created. See v. 18 and note.

Perhaps even more helpful is an understanding of "firstborn" from the OT. For example, Ps 89:27 celebrates King David as "the firstborn, the highest of the kings of the earth." Obviously David was not the first king on earth or even the first in Israel, a title that belongs to King Saul (1Sm 10). Also, we know that David was not even the firstborn son in his family (1Sm 16:10–13). From these points, we begin rightly to understand that "firstborn" was a title and not just a literal description of when someone was born. (Elsewhere in the Bible "firstborn" means "one who is privileged" [e.g., Ex 4:22]). David was called firstborn because God declared him to be the inheritor of Israel's throne. Jesus is firstborn because the heavenly Father declares Him to be the ruler of all creation. This expression was probably more common in biblical times when being the first or having the title of firstborn gave one the lion's share of the family inheritance.

1:16 *all things.* Paul's point about the uniqueness of Jesus and His reign are further described. As Creator of "all things," Jesus is supreme over all (Jn 1:3). *invisible.* There's more here than meets the eye—Paul did not just refer to physical things like air and wind that are felt but not seen. This expression included spiritual creatures such as the angels, as Christians still say today in the Nicene Creed that God is the "maker . . . of all things visible and invisible" and think of angelic beings. The Colossians were particularly interested in angels as we shall see in ch. 2. However, Paul asserted Jesus' supremacy over the invisible angels. *thrones . . . dominions . . . rulers . . . authorities.* Some interpreters think that these and similar terms refer to personal beings, such as angels (fallen or otherwise; cf. Eph 1:21; 6:12). Others identify these with the impersonal orders (e.g., government) that structure the created universe. It seems preferable not to draw a hard and fast distinction between these two possibilities. Since God created both the personal and impersonal "powers," and since both are subject to corruption as a result of sin, it is very likely that the terms have a broad point of reference. They refer to the angelic and especially demonic beings (fallen angels); the fallen angelic powers attempt to use the various orders of creation as tools in their endeavors to move people to put their faith and hope elsewhere than in Christ. The names that Paul used here for angelic or demonic beings are all found in Jewish literature of the intertestamental period as well as in the NT. Some people in intertestamental times and NT times thought that such spiritual "powers" controlled the universe. The false teachers present at Colossae apparently assigned to them power independent of Christ (2:8) and held them to be objects of worship (2:18). However, since Christ created them, they are subservient to Him. *through Him and for Him.* The goal of creation is the redemption that Christ accomplishes; He redeems the creation from the futility that resulted from the Fall (Gn 3:17–18) and in the life to come restores it to what its Creator intended for it (Rm 8:19–22). Another way in which the NT teaches these truths is found in those passages that make use of "new creation" language (e.g., 2Co 5:17; Rv 21:1–22:5; see also hymns such as *LSB* 387; H82 100; TPH 40; TUMH 246; and *LSB* 817; H82 412; TPH 458); this is also the message of the "miracles of nature" that Jesus performed (e.g., Mt 14:13–21; Jn 6:15–21). Our salvation through Christ is the restoration of the goodness of the original creation (Gn 1:31). Christ's forgiveness remedies all the corruption that came upon the created universe as a result of mankind's fall into sin (e.g., Gn 3:16–19). We know this blessing now by faith as we experience it through Christ's Word and His Sacraments (e.g., Col 1:25–27; 2:12; Mt 26:29). In the resurrection to eternal life we will know it by sight (see *LSB* 720; H82 209; TPH 399). See further the note on "reconcile" at 1:20.

1:17 *He is before all things.* "His beloved Son" (v. 13) existed before the creation (Jn 1:1–2; 3:16). This is another reason for understanding "firstborn" in 1:15 as designating Christ as the eternal Creator of all things and not as the first of everything that was created. *in Him all things hold together.* This speaks against the heretical teaching that the creation or physical matter is inherently evil. In a materialistic culture like we have today, people rarely fall into this false teaching—indeed, we are often more in danger of focusing so completely on physical and material things that we forget the spiritual! But sometimes as persons seek to grow spiritually and as they struggle against the lusts of the body, these old ideas crop up in them. We do well to remember that God created all things good (Gn 1:31) and that, since the fall into sin, even the spiritual aspects of human life are corrupted (Mt 15:19). We need redemption for both body and soul. Jesus still cares very much about this created world, continues to sustain it, and will renew it. Thus we turn to Him for our physical and other needs for this life as well as for our eternal needs pertaining to the life to come.

1:18 *head of His body, the church.* This phrase occurs in the first subsection of the hymn, which deals with creation (see the introduction to this section). However, its content plainly points to the theme of the second subsection of the hymn: reconciliation. The phrase serves to unite the themes of creation and reconciliation or new creation (see the note on "reconcile" at 1:20). *head.* Paul described Jesus' relationship to the Church using his common imagery of the human body and human relationships (cf. Eph 5:23). In the OT, the word for head is commonly used to describe a variety of leaders. But Paul made clear here that Jesus does not give His office and calling to anyone else since everyone else is naturally different from the eternal Christ through whom all things were made. This headship over the Church became an issue in the Early Church as bishops vied for priority. The same thing happened during the Middle Ages as the bishop of Rome asserted his authority over against political and national leaders. At that time many rulers wanted to be the head of the churches in their realms, which naturally interfered with the service of the bishops. While the reformers recognized the proper authority of both king and pope, they guarded against understanding the papacy as the supreme authority in the Church. They wrote, "The pope is not, according to divine law or God's Word, the head of all

Christendom. This name belongs to One only, whose name is Jesus Christ" (SA II IV 1). *body*. The language of "head" and "body" (unique to Paul among NT writers) indicates the intimate relationship between the Redeemer and the redeemed. The concept is similar to what Paul taught with the "in Christ" terminology (see note at 1:2). This relationship is created in Baptism (2:11–13; see also 1Co 12:12; Gal 3:27–28) and sustained in the Lord's Supper (1Co 10:16–17). See further the notes at 1:24; 2:10, 19; 3:15. Knox observed,

> St. Paul calls the congregation the body of Christ, whereof every one of us is a member, teaching us thereby that no member is of sufficiency to sustain and feed himself without the help and support of any other. (Knox 214)

church. The Greek term is *ekklesia*, from which we get words such as "ecclesiastical." In the NT it most often denotes a local Christian congregation (e.g., 1Co 4:17) but can describe the Church at large (Eph 1:22). In secular Greek the word referred to any public assembly (it is so translated in Ac 19:32); in the Greek translation of the OT it was used to render Hebrew words referring to Israel as God's chosen people. This dual Greek and Old Testament background to *ekklesia* made it well suited to describe the community of the followers of Jesus Christ: it is the continuation of Israel as the people of God, **and** it is an assembly that is open to anyone who embraces Jesus as Savior and Lord through faith in Him. It can be difficult for us today to appreciate how profound a change this was for the first Christians. They had grown up in a Jewish world where Gentiles were often literally the enemy or at least a defiling presence in their midst. What the Lord accomplished in changing their views in those early centuries is truly amazing and a point of reflection for us as we use the word "church" and confess "one holy Christian and apostolic Church" in a global environment with profound diversity. *firstborn from the dead*. Just as Jesus is the "firstborn of all creation/every creature" (v. 15) and thus the cause of creation, so He is also the cause of the resurrection (cf. Rm 8:29; 1Co 15:20–21). As we noted above that "firstborn" was a title and not necessarily the first instance of something, so here one may note that other people were raised from the dead before Jesus was (e.g., 2Ki 13:21; Lk 7:11–17; Jn 11:38–44). He is Lord over life and over death.

1:19 *fullness of God*. Col 2:9 states explicitly what is implied here; namely, that the eternal God, who does not have a body or other material existence, began to dwell in the body of the child Jesus of Nazareth. The totality of God with all His divine attributes began to dwell in Christ at the moment of His conception by the Holy Spirit of the Virgin Mary. This mystery, that the non-corporal and invisible God became a corporal and visible man, can only be comprehended in light of the biblical truths of the Holy Trinity (that God is three distinct persons in one divine being) and of the two natures in Christ (that Jesus is both fully God and fully man (as described in the Athanasian Creed). See further 2:9, which indicates that the fullness which began to dwell in Christ at the incarnation continues to dwell in Him for all time.

One should not overlook the fact that Paul wrote here of a paradox as surprising as the one he described in v. 15 when he stated that Jesus "is the image of the invisible God." For the Lord declared through the prophet Jeremiah, "Do I not fill heaven and earth?" (23:24). When reading that the fullness of God dwelt in one man, one gets wild mental pictures of the entire universe collapsing into something the size of the human body—mountains, oceans, plants, stars, and galaxies pour in and compress until nothing is left but One shining brightly against the abyss. However, such a mental picture fails to do justice to the mystery that Paul referenced, since what we imagine envisions physical things, whereas Paul was writing about a spiritual reality beyond our comprehending. He wrote about the fullness of God, not the universe full of things. Somehow God's fullness dwells in Jesus of Nazareth, through whom He made all and holds all together.

1:20 *reconcile*. Sin alienated the creation from the Creator. Christ reconciles "all things," i.e., He brings everything back to its proper order, namely, the same harmonious relationship with God the Creator that the creation (human and non-human) had before the fall into sin and the corruption that resulted from it. This reconciliation and restoration that Christ accomplishes is often depicted in the Scriptures by "new creation" language, by language that speaks of the creation being restored to its original, right relationship with God (Am 9:13 and Rv 21:1 would be examples of such "new creation" language). See also the notes at 1:16 and 22. *making peace*. Jesus' death makes peace between God and mankind possible; such peace is personally experienced only through faith (see 1:23). Christ's death on the cross is also His victory over all who continue to oppose

Him (see further 2:16–23 and the notes there; see also 1Co 15:26–28; Eph 2:14–16). *On earth or in heaven*. The phrase is repeated from v. 16, but the order is reversed. This reversal of the order serves to emphasize that in reconciling humans to God, Christ also restores the creation to what God intended for it. The Lord of hosts is a God of order who arranged the elements of His good creation and rearranges the elements of the fallen creation so that it again bears His divine imprint and is blessed with the goodness in Christ. *blood of His cross*. Those crucified generally died by suffocation due to the collapse of the chest muscles. Therefore, the apostle's mention of the "blood" of our Lord's cross is intentional and emphatic. Although each of the Gospel writers referenced the shedding of Jesus' blood in some way (most consistently with the Last Supper), it was the apostle John who told us that one of the soldiers pierced Jesus' side so that His blood poured forth freely in testimony to His death. As with the Gospel writers, Paul's mention of "blood" recalled the OT sacrificial system, in which the blood of sacrificial animals was offered as payment for sin to secure forgiveness. In a similar way Christ's death is the payment for the forgiveness of the entire world once and for all. The reconciliation and peace Paul described are accomplished facts.

1:15–20 in Devotion and Prayer How can we sinners be sure that Christ's work reconciles us to God? The firstborn of creation who is also the firstborn of the new creation was Paul's answer. He made his argument with two paradoxes: one of sight and one of size. Jesus shows what we cannot see. Jesus holds in His conceived, born, and resurrected body what all the universe cannot contain. In Him one sees God and meets Him in His fullness. Paul said we have assurance in God's presence because of who Christ is: the image of the invisible God—that is, He is both the Creator and the Reconciler, who holds everything together. • "Praise be to Him who, Lord Most High, The fullness of the Godhead shares; And yet our human nature bears, Who came as man to bleed and die. And from His cross there flows our peace Who chose for us the path He trod, That so might sins and sorrows cease And all be reconciled to God." (*LSB* 538:3)

Main Exposition and Resolution (1:21–2:23)

Ministry of reconciliation (1:21–29)

ESV	KJV
[21]And you, who once were alienated and hostile in mind, doing evil deeds, [22]he has now reconciled in his body of flesh by his death, in order to present you holy and blameless and above reproach before him, [23]if indeed you continue in the faith, stable and steadfast, not shifting from the hope of the gospel that you heard, which has been proclaimed in all creation under heaven, and of which I, Paul, became a minister. [24]Now I rejoice in my sufferings for your sake, and in my flesh I am filling up what is lacking in Christ's afflictions for the sake of his body, that is, the church, [25]of which I became a minister according to the stewardship from God that was given to me for you, to make the word of God fully known, [26]the mystery hidden for ages and generations but now revealed to his saints. [27]To them God chose to make known how great among the Gentiles are the riches of the glory of this mystery, which is Christ in you, the hope of glory. [28]Him we proclaim, warning everyone and teaching everyone with all wisdom, that we may present everyone mature in Christ. [29]For this I toil, struggling with all his energy that he powerfully works within me.	[21]And you, that were sometime alienated and enemies in your mind by wicked works, yet now hath he reconciled [22]In the body of his flesh through death, to present you holy and unblameable and unreproveable in his sight: [23]If ye continue in the faith grounded and settled, and be not moved away from the hope of the gospel, which ye have heard, and which was preached to every creature which is under heaven; whereof I Paul am made a minister; [24]Who now rejoice in my sufferings for you, and fill up that which is behind of the afflictions of Christ in my flesh for his body's sake, which is the church: [25]Whereof I am made a minister, according to the dispensation of God which is given to me for you, to fulfil the word of God; [26]Even the mystery which hath been hid from ages and from generations, but now is made manifest to his saints: [27]To whom God would make known what is the riches of the glory of this mystery among the Gentiles; which is Christ in you, the hope of glory: [28]Whom we preach, warning every man, and teaching every man in all wisdom; that we may present every man perfect in Christ Jesus: [29]Whereunto I also labour, striving according to his working, which worketh in me mightily.

31

Introduction to 1:21–29 Here Paul moved from the "Overture" to the main exposition of the letter. With these verses his topic of discussion also transitioned from the work of Christ for all to the ministry of the Word that brings the blessings of Christ to us personally. This profound exposition of the ministry of the Word also led the apostle to speak of the role of suffering in the life of God's people.

1:21 *you.* This word designates Paul's readers as believers, who nevertheless had previously been alienated from God (Eph 4:18). *alienated and hostile.* Our hostility toward God was a result of our sinfulness; our sinfulness and hostility could be seen in the evil deeds we did. Our sinfulness alienated us from God and His benefits. *in mind.* In many NT passages, such as this one, the "mind" indicates that which controls all one's actions and indeed one's entire being. In colloquial fashion it might be said that we were "rotten to the core."

1:22 *reconciled.* Reconciliation is the repairing of broken relations, and hence the restoring to us of that favorable relationship with God with which He first created mankind. The past tense of the verb "reconciled" indicates that this reconciliation is completed in Christ's work. Reconciliation is not something Christ has started and we need to complete. *in His body.* The false teachers taught that salvation came through knowledge. Paul emphasized that salvation came from God, specifically through the incarnation, through Jesus' physical life, death, and resurrection (cf. 1Tm 2:5; 1Jn 4:2). *holy.* See the note on "saints" at 1:2. *above reproach.* This means unaccused, free of charges. Paul had in mind the whole picture of life with God: our justification (declared righteousness, forgiveness; Rm 3:23–26), our baptismal life on earth (sanctification; Rm 6–7), and our ultimate glorification (life in heaven; Rm 8). The three terms "holy," "blameless," and "beyond reproach" are synonyms; the apostle used all three here to emphasize the majesty of the salvation Christ has won for us.

1:23 *continue.* Paul first hinted at the problem facing the church at Colossae: the temptation to turn away from faith in Christ. His readers would forfeit their salvation if they were to stop trusting in Christ. Faith in Christ must continue just as it began—by hearing the Gospel (Jn 8:31–32; Rm 10:17). For that reason this section contains numerous references to the Gospel and its proclamation (23, 25, 26, 27, 28). *proclaimed in all creation.* Jesus promised that the Gospel would be proclaimed throughout the whole world (Mt 24:14). Earlier, Paul said the Gospel had come to the whole world (v. 6). He made similar statements about his ministry in Rm 15:19 and 2Tm 4:17. These statements are all in harmony with the message of the Book of Acts, which presents the apostle's unhindered preaching of the Gospel in Rome, the capital of the NT world, as the fulfillment of the promise of Jesus that His followers would be His witnesses "unto the end of the earth" (Ac 1:8; 28:30–31). The universal scope of the Gospel is in contrast to the message of the false teachers that their secret knowledge was for the select few who could attain it. *minister.* See also the note at 1:7. Paul was completely bound in his service to the Gospel. He styled himself a minister of the Gospel, for that is how he served. In 1:25 he called himself a minister of the Church, for that is whom he served.

1:24 *sufferings . . . lacking in Christ's afflictions.* Some would understand "Christ's afflictions" as a synonym for "the sufferings of Christians." Hence, they would find the key to the understanding of this passage in 1Co 12:26, "If one member [of the church] suffers, all suffer together." They would suggest that the apostle is saying that he suffered with his readers, and perhaps that his bearing of sufferings helped them to bear their sufferings. Certainly 1Co 12:26 has some bearing on the correct interpretation of this admittedly difficult passage.

Nevertheless, Paul spoke of "Christ's afflictions" rather than simply the afflictions of Christians. It seems better to look also for interpretive help to those passages that speak of Christians sharing in Christ's sufferings. We note, first of all, that Christ's sufferings for our salvation are complete (vv. 20, 22; 2:9–15). Furthermore, the term that the apostle used here, "afflictions," is never used by any NT author for the redemptive work of our Lord. Therefore, this passage is not maintaining that there is anything in Christ's redemptive work that needs completing. In fact, such an idea would fly in the face of the entire NT!

This helps us to see that the "afflictions" that Paul mentioned here are those things that all Christians suffer with Christ (2Tm 3:12; Rm 8:17) because we are "His body." Christians suffer on account of (1) their faith in Christ, (2) their new life of godly living for Christ, and/or (3) their witness to Christ. As Baptism connects us to the death and resurrection of Christ for our salvation and makes us members of His body, so it also connects us to the sufferings of Christ, which we experience for the sake of our faith, service, and witness (Col 2:12; Rm 6:3–8; Php 3:10). Paul gladly accepted such suffering for the sake of the Gospel (Php 2:17) and understood that it brought benefits to the Church (2Co 1:5–7; 4:10–12; Eph 3:13).

Therefore, the apostle meant to teach the following: In the church at Colossae are those who have begun to withdraw from their faith in Christ. If they reduce their faith, they will reduce their service and witness as well. Such a decrease in faith/service/witness will inevitably result in a decrease in suffering with Christ. In view of the Colossians' wavering, Paul was moved to increase his witness to the Gospel (such as through the composition and sending of this Letter). This increase in witness brought with it an increase in the apostle's suffering of "the afflictions of Christ." Paul chose to suffer on behalf of the Colossian Christians ("for the sake of his body, that is, the church"). What he did for them is an example of the truth of 1Co 12:26 in action.

1:25 *minister.* See the notes at 1:7 and 1:23. *stewardship.* The Greek term is *oikonomia*, "management," "plan," from which English "economy" derives. Paul used this word to describe God's overall plan of salvation as He guides history (Eph 1:10) and also to refer to the management plan entrusted to individual ministers of the Word (1Co 9:17). While both of these uses are pertinent to the understanding of this passage, the ministry of the Word is the primary reference here. *to make the word of God fully known.* This could refer to the completeness of the Gospel message in contrast to the claims of the false teachers, who taught that God's earlier revelation was deficient (cf. Mt 28:19–20, "all that I have commanded you"). However, it seems more likely that the apostle is here hearkening back to the statement of 1:23 concerning the universal scope of the Gospel. See the fuller discussion at 1:23.

1:26 *mystery.* Paul used the Greek term *mysterion* far more often than any other NT writer. A mystery is something hidden, although it may be made known through revelation (Rm 16:25; Eph 3:3). God kept the mystery hidden during OT times (although it was present in shadows and types, see 2:17 and note), but the ministry of Christ revealed it ("now"). The apostle used the word of God's plan of salvation (1:25) to reveal the mystery.

In a skillfully written mystery novel (those of Agatha Christie come to mind) there will be a variety of facts in the story whose significance will be hidden from the reader until the outcome of the story is revealed (generally involving the identity of the culprit and how he/she went about accomplishing the deed). By re-reading the novel, the reader will be able to pick up on the significance of these facts, both small and great, that at first seemed insignificant. In a comparable way, the significance of many portions of the OT were hidden until the ministry of Christ revealed their significance. (Another apostle testified that the OT prophets themselves had to examine their own prophecies of salvation as they sought for a deeper understanding of the truths to which the Holy Spirit was bearing witness through them; 1Pt 1:10–12.) But now God has revealed the mystery of salvation in Christ. We are privileged to live after the time of this revelation! We may now examine the OT Scriptures to discover the meaning of those things that were a mystery to the prophets and other OT believers. See further 1:27; 2:2 and the notes there.

saints. In the Scriptures this term refers to those who are holy before God by way of the forgiveness of their sins through faith in Christ. See also the note at 1:2.

1:27 *Christ in you*. The mystery is not only about Christ coming to this world but also about Christ coming personally to us through Word and Sacrament (Rm 8:10). As the Greek for "you" here and in 3:16 is in the plural, the stress is on Christ's dwelling among His believers through Word and Sacrament. Hence, "Christ among you" would also be an acceptable translation. See further the note at 3:16. *the hope of glory*. On "hope," see 1:5 and the note there. The term "glory" in Pauline usage is rich with meaning. It can refer to the being of God Himself (Rm 1:23; 1Co 2:8). This is in keeping with the use of the Hebrew equivalent in the OT to designate the presence of God (e.g., Ex 16:7). It is comparable in meaning to the "image" of God (2Co 3:18). "Glory" is also used to describe the splendor of eternal life (2Co 3:8–11). All of this makes "glory" a significant term to designate the content of the Gospel (2Co 4:4).

1:28 *Him we proclaim*. This is a succinct summary of the mission of the Church and the heart of the biblical message. Christ is all our focus. *warning . . . teaching*. The word "teaching" points to the entirety of the biblical message (Mt 28:19), while "warning" puts some emphasis upon admonition (Ti 3:10). Taken together, the terms point to the Law and Gospel outline of the Christian message ("repentance and forgiveness of sins," Lk 24:47). *mature*. The Greek term can also be translated "perfect" or "complete." Only by virtue of a saving rela-

35

tionship with Christ can we be what God wants us to be. He would restore us to the perfection in which He created us.

1:29 *His energy.* A more literal translation might be "His working that is working in me." Cf. 2:12; Php 4:13. God is the source for ministry in the Gospel as He provides the power for faith and salvation and for the ability to live by faith.

1:21–29 in Devotion and Prayer How can we sinners be sure that we have the reconciliation with God that Christ acquired by His redemptive work? Paul points us to the ministry of the Gospel, through which God works powerfully to reconcile us to Himself. The word of Christ gives us all the assurance concerning our salvation that we need. All people suffer because of the fallen nature of the world. But Christians are called to a special form of suffering for the sake of Christ: rejection, ridicule, and persecution. No one likes suffering. Nevertheless, the tears of Christian suffering reflect the glory of the cross of Christ. Remember how God used Christ's sufferings to save us. He will also use our sufferings to bring Christ's saving work to others who have no hope. • "In suff'ring be Thy love my peace, In weakness be Thy love my pow'r; And when the storms of life shall cease, O Jesus, in that final hour, Be Thou my rod and staff and guide, And draw me safely to Thy side!" Amen. (*LSB* 683:4)

True knowledge (2:1–5)

ESV	KJV
2 ¹For I want you to know how great a struggle I have for you and for those at Laodicea and for all who have not seen me face to face, ²that their hearts may be encouraged, being knit together in love, to reach all the riches of full assurance of understanding and the knowledge of God's mystery, which is Christ, ³in whom are hidden all the treasures of wisdom and knowledge. ⁴I say this in order that no one may delude you with plausible arguments. ⁵For though I am absent in body, yet I am with you in spirit, rejoicing to see your good order and the firmness of your faith in Christ.	2 ¹For I would that ye knew what great conflict I have for you, and for them at Laodicea, and for as many as have not seen my face in the flesh; ²That their hearts might be comforted, being knit together in love, and unto all riches of the full assurance of understanding, to the acknowledgement of the mystery of God, and of the Father, and of Christ; ³In whom are hid all the treasures of wisdom and knowledge. ⁴And this I say, lest any man should beguile you with enticing words. ⁵For though I be absent in the flesh, yet am I with you in the spirit, joying and beholding your order, and the steadfastness of your faith in Christ.

Introduction to 2:1–5 Paul here again took up the topics of true wisdom/knowledge/understanding. He did so because here he also first began to make specific evaluations and criticisms of the false teaching that was enticing his readers.

2:1 *struggle.* The Greek term is *agona*, from which comes the English "agony." Paul showed great pastoral concern for his readers' spiritual welfare. Theological errors are not to be overlooked or expected to go away on their own. *Laodicea.* This was a town about 11 mi from Colossae. The close associations that this Letter makes between these two cities suggest that they were closely related to one another. Epaphras (1:7) may well have been the founding missionary and pastor of both churches. See also 4:13, 15, 16 and the notes there. *in the flesh.* The KJV provides a most literal translation of the Greek.

2:2 *hearts* In biblical vocabulary "heart" refers to one's true, inner being in its spiritual, mental, and emotional dimensions. *knit together in love.* This phrase can also mean "instructed in love." Paul may well have written in a way that reached for both meanings of this expression. He was saying that the Colossians had been instructed in the love that God showed them in Christ, and that this instruction motivated and empowered them to be knit together in Christ-like love for one another. Our own efforts do not produce our love and unity, but God's love in Jesus generates these gifts. *assurance.* Their assurance of salvation is based on the power of God's true Word (1Th 1:5); that was a major emphasis of 1:25–28. Luther wrote of this verse, "He has overwhelmed us with unspeakable, eternal treasures by His Son and the Holy Spirit" (LC II 24). *mystery.* See the notes at 1:26 and 1:27. *and of the Father.* Many Greek manuscripts have this phrase found in the KJV. Scribes often sought to clarify which divine person(s) were meant by the word "God," similar to the way we might provide a parenthesis identifying someone's name.

2:3 *hidden.* Here the term does not mean "hidden from view," for it was a contention of the false teachers that the deep mysteries of wisdom and knowledge were hidden from most. Rather, here the word means "guarded for safekeeping." Paul challenged the false teachers, who claimed special insight into the mysteries of God. All that we can and need to know about God is ultimately revealed to us in Christ.

2:4 *no one.* Paul left no room for error, because such error is a persuasive deception that would lead people away from Christ. *plausible arguments.* It appears that the attraction of the heresy present at Colossae sprang at least partially from the impressive sounding rhetoric that the false teachers employed. Throughout history, silver-throated oratory and dynamic public speaking have often been used to promote falsehood.

2:5 *with you in spirit.* The Greek of the NT does not distinguish by capital and lower case between the Holy Spirit and the human spirit on which the Holy Spirit works (Rm 8:16). Only the context can help the reader decide whether "Spirit" or "spirit" is the correct English translation. Further the human "spirit" sometimes refers simply to one's inner thoughts (1Co 2:11). The apostle might simply have meant that he was present with his readers "in my mind," in sentiment." However, it is possible that he meant instead (or also) that since the Holy Spirit ministers to our spirits through the Word, both Paul and his hearers were united by their mutual attention to God's Word in Christ. 1Co 5:3 provides the most helpful parallel in Paul's writing, which is why the translators view this as a reference to Paul's spirit. *good order . . . firmness.* These terms have military associations. God's gifts resist incursions of false teachings in the Church. Although there are temptations and dangers to faith plaguing the Colossians, at this point they had not yet fallen completely out of faith in Christ. They were still resisting the appeal of the false teaching.

2:1–5 in Devotion and Prayer Whatever this false teaching was that had infiltrated the Colossian church, it was not the teaching of Jesus Christ. We, too, can be drawn away from Christ by all sorts of attractive thoughts and words. Eventually, Christ-less or Christ-lite teachings will separate us from God and from one another. But the treasures of His wisdom and knowledge overcome all temptation and defeat all deception. His words will always encourage us and strengthen us in faith and love. • Grant, O Lord, that Your Word among us may be taught in its truth and purity in Christ, and protect us from those who would do otherwise. Fill us with full assurance of understanding and knowledge of the Christ, our only Savior. Amen.

The fullness of Christ (2:6–15)

ESV	KJV
⁶Therefore, as you received Christ Jesus the Lord, so walk in him, ⁷rooted and built up in him and established in the faith, just as you were taught, abounding in thanksgiving. ⁸See to it that no one takes you captive by philosophy and empty deceit, according to human tradition, according to the elemental spirits of the world, and not according to Christ. ⁹For in him the whole fullness of deity dwells bodily, ¹⁰and you have been filled in him, who is the head of all rule and authority. ¹¹In him also you were circumcised with a circumcision made without hands, by putting off the body of the flesh, by the circumcision of Christ, ¹²having been buried with him in baptism, in which you were also raised with him through faith in the powerful working of God, who raised him from the dead. ¹³And you, who were dead in your trespasses and the uncircumcision of your flesh, God made alive together with him, having forgiven us all our trespasses, ¹⁴by canceling the record of debt that stood against us with its legal demands. This he set aside, nailing it to the cross. ¹⁵He disarmed the rulers and authorities and put them to open shame, by triumphing over them in him.	⁶As ye have therefore received Christ Jesus the Lord, so walk ye in him: ⁷Rooted and built up in him, and stablished in the faith, as ye have been taught, abounding therein with thanksgiving. ⁸Beware lest any man spoil you through philosophy and vain deceit, after the tradition of men, after the rudiments of the world, and not after Christ. ⁹For in him dwelleth all the fulness of the Godhead bodily. ¹⁰And ye are complete in him, which is the head of all principality and power: ¹¹In whom also ye are circumcised with the circumcision made without hands, in putting off the body of the sins of the flesh by the circumcision of Christ: ¹²Buried with him in baptism, wherein also ye are risen with him through the faith of the operation of God, who hath raised him from the dead. ¹³And you, being dead in your sins and the uncircumcision of your flesh, hath he quickened together with him, having forgiven you all trespasses; ¹⁴Blotting out the handwriting of ordinances that was against us, which was contrary to us, and took it out of the way, nailing it to his cross; ¹⁵And having spoiled principalities and powers, he made a shew of them openly, triumphing over them in it.

Introduction to 2:6–15 In this section Paul offered as profound and exalted a description of Christ and His work as we find anywhere in Scripture. He noted that the work of Christ for our forgiveness also involves triumph over the "powers" of creation that the Colossians were being tempted to follow. He also made explicit reference to the role of Baptism in all of this.

2:6 *Christ Jesus the Lord*. This phrase recalls the earliest Christian baptismal confession (Rm 10:9; 1Co 12:3). Hence, the Colossians "received Christ Jesus the Lord" in their Baptism (2:12). *walk in Him*. "Walk" is a common Biblical term to refer to ethical conduct, to one's "way of life" (Eph 4:1, 17; 5:2; 1Th 4:1).

2:7 *rooted and built up*. These are both metaphors, one from nature and the other from construction. They point to something that is firm and enduring. This verse and the previous verse demonstrate that such firmness in the Christian faith and in living the Christian life comes from God's Word. For God's Word, centered in Christ, is the content of what the Colossians "received" and "were taught." Both of these verbs describe the proclamation of the whole of God's Word. The Colossians "received" the teachings the way one might receive family "traditions" (meaning "that which is handed over and received"). See further the note at 2Th 2:15).

2:8 *philosophy and empty deceit*. In NT times "philosophy" was a broad term that could refer to a variety of points of view and to abilities, whether academic or practical for life. Such human wisdom can help us with many questions but it is powerless to explain God adequately. If we think it can, we are deceived. The word "deceit" is not limited to deliberate attempts to deceive. It can also refer to those who are sincere in what they do but are in error and so lead others astray. *human tradition*. The Greek term "tradition," along with the Greek words for "give" and "received" that are derived from it, are sometimes used in the NT to designate the truth of Christian doctrine (1Co 11:2). Here the adjective "human" makes it plain that the apostle was referring to ideas of human origin rather than to teachings God revealed in His Word. See further the note at 2Th 2:15. *elemental spirits*. This term can refer to the basic elements of the (fallen) universe; something along these lines is the meaning of the word in Gal 4:3, 9. In Colossians this term is also used of the fallen angels (vv. 18–20), and so also designates false teachings. See the note at 1:16.

2:9 *fullness*. This was a technical term in later Gnosticism for a number of pseudo-divine beings that supposedly emanated from God (angels, rulers, authorities, thrones, dominions). The term may have been used in the same way by the heretics at Colossae. Against this, Paul taught that everything that is of God dwells in Christ. Paul included the term "deity" here to make explicit something he referred to in the companion passage of 1:19, namely that the term "fullness" designates the wholeness of the Deity. Whatever makes God to be God dwells in Jesus Christ and dwells in Him **bodily**. Christians have confessed this in the Nicene Creed since the fourth century: "[Christ is] very God of very God . . . being of one substance with the Father." The Lutheran reformers marveled, "In this personal union the two natures have such a grand, intimate, indescribable communion that even the angels are astonished by it" (FC SD VIII 30). *dwells bodily*. Jesus of Nazareth is God in the flesh. The present tense of the verb "dwells" indicates that Christ continues to dwell with His human body as both God and man for all eternity. This passage also refutes the Colossian heretics' principle that the flesh/human body is evil.

2:10 *filled*. Another translation would be "completed." Christians have everything they need in Christ. The play on words between "filled" and "fullness" points to the truth that in redeeming us, God makes us to be like Christ. Chemnitz wrote,

> All these blessings, I say, in perfect and complete fullness we have in Christ, who for us became incarnate, was crucified, and rose again; so that as from our Head to us as members all these blessings are distributed and flow and are given as our help from His fullness. As a result of this Paul concludes that there is no need of any of the other elements of this world for our salvation, since we possess His fullness in Christ (Chemnitz 6:314).

As we read in 2Pt 1:4, the redemption accomplished by Christ makes us "partakers of the divine nature" since we are the body of Christ, our head (See also Ap V 58.)

2:11 *circumcision*. Circumcision was a sign of God's covenant establishing the people of Israel (Gn 17:9). But in Christ the purpose of the covenant with Abraham (to be a blessing to all the families of the earth; Gn 12:3) was fulfilled. The new covenant is established with a different circumcision, one made through divine means: Baptism. Since the Israelite circumcision was performed on the eighth day after birth, this verse points to the validity of infant Baptism. The Scriptures (e.g., Ps 51:5) refute the notion that God regards children as innocent before the application of the Word and Baptism (see also FC Ep XII 6).

2:12 *buried . . . raised*. The same powerful working of God that raised Jesus from the dead is at work in Baptism. Baptism puts to death the sinful nature (Rm 6:6) and resurrects us in faith to a new life in Christ. Melanchthon observed, "When Paul describes conversion or renewal, he almost everywhere designates these two parts, *making dead and making alive*" (Ap XIIA 46). Also, "Faith is powerful through the power of God and overcomes death" (Ap V 129). Baptism makes us partakers with Christ in those things that He accomplished for our salvation (e.g., 1Co 15:3–4). Through the power of God, Baptism actually accomplishes these things ("Baptism . . . now saves you"; 1Pt 3:21). Therefore, Baptism is more than a symbol of what God does through the teaching of God's Word and through faith. Baptism is water combined with God's Word. That makes it a washing of regeneration (Ti 3:5–7). Wesley noted,

> The ancient manner of baptizing by immersion is as manifestly alluded to here, as the other manner of baptizing by sprinkling or pouring of water is, Heb 10:22. But no stress is laid on the age of the baptized, or the manner of performing it, in one or the other place. (Wesley 520)

2:13 *dead.* All people are born spiritually dead (see also Eph 2:1). Though they were created for fellowship with God, they are separated from Him. *your trespasses and the uncircumcision.* Our problem before God is not only the individual sins (trespasses) that we commit, it is also the corruption of our entire being by sin (here designated by the phrase "uncircumcision of your flesh"). Even though the individual sins that one man commits might seem to be less than the sins of others, the corruption of his being by sin ("uncircumcision") makes him just as much in need of forgiveness as anyone else. God removed this "uncircumcision" in Baptism, through which He forgives our sinfulness. *forgiven us.* Our trespasses are the cause of our spiritual death. God made us alive from this spiritual death through forgiving our trespasses. The spiritual deliverance results in our deliverance from eternal death for eternal life.

2:14 *record . . . legal demands.* In the first century, the creditor kept a handwritten bill of indebtedness. In this case, the "record of debt" is the record of all our violations of God's Law. This record is wiped away by Jesus' death on the cross. This vivid word-picture derives from the manner of our Lord's death: He was crucified with the charge against Him posted above His head on a tablet that could be erased or blotted over (Mt 27:37; Mk 15:26; Lk 23:38; Jn 19:19–22). *that stood against us.* In contrast with the literal phrase by phrase translation in the KJV, the ESV combines the emphatic "that was against us, which was contrary to us" into a single, simpler expression. *nailing*. This verse joins Jn 20:25 as the only NT passages that specify that Jesus was nailed to the cross. Together these verses offer an intriguing possibility for the interpretation of Is 49:15–16, the promise of the Lord to His people, "I will not forget you. Behold, I have engraved you on the palms of My hands."

2:15 *rulers and authorities*. These are created by God and yet are often corrupted by sin. They can be personal (such as angels) or impersonal (such as governments, economic systems, educational institutions). They might also be demons masquerading as idols or false gods (1Co 10:19–20). See also the notes at 1:16 and 2:9. *triumphing*. Paul had in mind the Roman custom of stripping defeated armies of weapons and armor and parading them in a triumphal procession. Since Christ has defeated these "rulers," Christians should not feel tempted to follow them, nor should they feel threatened by them. In most places in the world and in most eras in history, people have been plagued by a great fear of the demonic; hence, Luther's famous hymn stanza "Though devils all the world should fill All eager to devour us" (*LSB* 656:3; H82 687:3; TPH 260:3; TUMH 110:3). The victory over the demonic, wrought by Christ and proclaimed in passages such as this one, gave Christians a sense of victory over Satan and therefore assuaged their fears of the demonic. Luther's hymn continues "We tremble not, we fear no ill; They shall not overpow'r us." As Christianity became the dominant influence in Western culture, Western society in general lost its paralyzing fear of devils and demons. This freedom from feeling under the influence of demons largely endured, even after Christianity's place as the dominant influence in our society waned. Thus, the general lack of fear that our culture exhibits toward the demonic is a testimony to the victory of Christ over the fallen powers. Christianity has to a large extent "exorcized" our culture, though Christians should not be ignorant of Satan's continued influence. *in Him*. Since "God (the Father)" rather than "Christ" has been understood as the subject of the verbs since v. 13, and since the Greek prepositional phrase used here ("in Him") is regularly used in Paul's letters to denote the Christian's saving relationship with Christ, the translation "in Him" is to be preferred to "in it" (referring to the cross) as one finds in the KJV.

2:6–15 in Devotion and Prayer Seeking guidance and security from creation rather than from the Creator will end in disaster. We must not forget that sin has corrupted all creation. Created things, as good as they may be, are no substitute for God. He delivers us and gives us the forgiveness of sins in Jesus Christ. In Baptism, we have been raised up as a new creation. • "Satan, hear this proclamation: I am baptized into Christ! Drop your ugly accusation, I am not so soon enticed. Now that to the font I've traveled, All your might has come unraveled, And, against your tyranny, God, my Lord, unites with me!" Amen. (*LSB* 594:3)

True freedom (2:16–23)

ESV	KJV
¹⁶Therefore let no one pass judgment on you in questions of food and drink, or with regard to a festival or a new moon or a Sabbath. ¹⁷These are a shadow of the things to come, but the substance belongs to Christ. ¹⁸Let no one disqualify you, insisting on asceticism and worship of angels, going on in detail about visions, puffed up without reason by his sensuous mind, ¹⁹and not holding fast to the Head, from whom the whole body, nourished and knit together through its joints and ligaments, grows with a growth that is from God. ²⁰If with Christ you died to the elemental spirits of the world, why, as if you were still alive in the world, do you submit to regulations— ²¹"Do not handle, Do not taste, Do not touch" ²²(referring to things that all perish as they are used)—according to human precepts and teachings? ²³These have indeed an appearance of wisdom in promoting self-made religion and asceticism and severity to the body, but they are of no value in stopping the indulgence of the flesh.	¹⁶Let no man therefore judge you in meat, or in drink, or in respect of an holyday, or of the new moon, or of the sabbath days: ¹⁷Which are a shadow of things to come; but the body is of Christ. ¹⁸Let no man beguile you of your reward in a voluntary humility and worshipping of angels, intruding into those things which he hath not seen, vainly puffed up by his fleshly mind, ¹⁹And not holding the Head, from which all the body by joints and bands having nourishment ministered, and knit together, increaseth with the increase of God. ²⁰Wherefore if ye be dead with Christ from the rudiments of the world, why, as though living in the world, are ye subject to ordinances, ²¹(Touch not; taste not; handle not; ²²Which all are to perish with the using;) after the commandments and doctrines of men? ²³Which things have indeed a shew of wisdom in will worship, and humility, and neglecting of the body: not in any honour to the satisfying of the flesh.

Introduction to 2:16–23 In these verses Paul's critique of the false teaching that was enticing his readers focused on the freedom they had in Christ. The apostle exhorted the Colossians not to become enslaved to doctrines, practices, and "powers" from which their baptismal death with Christ had set them free.

2:16 Although it is difficult to understand exactly what the Colossian heretics required of their adherents, we can see that their demands included dietary rules (v. 21), ascetic practices (vv. 18, 23), and adherence to some sort of a cultic calendar (v. 16). *Sabbath*. The other practices that the apostle mentioned in this verse were observed in some pagan religions as well as in Judaism. However, as the Sabbath was a distinctively Jewish observance, the presence of this word here indicates that there was a Jewish element associated with the Colossian heresy. Bengel wrote,

> Christ, after that He Himself, the Lord of the Sabbath, had come, or else before His suffering, in no obscure language taught the liberty of the Sabbath; but He asserted it more openly by Paul after His resurrection. (Bengel 174)

Calvin explained,

> But some one will say, "We still keep up some observances of days." I answer, that we do not by any means observe days, as though there were any sacredness in holidays, or as though it were not lawful to labour upon them, but that respect is paid to government and order—not to days. (Calvin 192)

2:17 *shadow of the things to come.* Paul taught that certain OT events and practices pointed beyond themselves and found their full meaning and realization in Christ (Rm 15:4; 1Co 10:1–11). These events and practices sustained OT believers.

A Shadow of Things to Come

In the present passage the apostle speaks specifically of dietary practices and religious observances from the OT era. These practices had value for their time (they were, after all, instituted by God). But now that "the fullness of time" (Gal 4:4) had arrived with the coming of him in whom dwells "the whole fullness of deity" (Col 2:9), it would be misguided to devote the same attention to these practices as had been the case previously.

Consider the following: an engaged couple who must spend time apart might cherish each other's photo. But after they are married and living together, it would be out of place to devote the same attention to the photo. The former attention must be directed to the spouse. Paul instructs his readers to devote in a similar way all their faith and attention to the Christ to whom these OT worship practices pointed.

Verses 16 and 17 are among those Biblical passages that demonstrate that Christians are not obligated to observe the Sabbath, the seventh day of the week (Saturday), as God's people were commanded to do in OT times. Other passages that teach this truth include Gal 4:10–11 and Mt 12:1–8 (Mk 2:23–28; Lk 6:1–5). Melanchthon wrote, "Scripture itself has abolished the Sabbath Day. It teaches that since the Gospel has been revealed, all the ceremonies of Moses can be omitted" (AC XXVIII 59). Already in NT times Christ's followers were making the first day of the week, Sunday, their regular day for worship (Ac 20:7; 1Co 16:2; Rv 1:10) in recognition that this was the day their Lord completed the work of salvation by rising from the dead (Mt 28:1; Lk 24:1; Jn 20:1, 19). Furthermore, these biblical texts make it plain that while God has commanded His people of NT times to gather together for public worship (Heb 10:25), He has not commanded that this must take place on Sunday or on any other specific day of the week (hence, it is misleading to speak of Sunday as "the Christian Sabbath." Nonetheless, two millennia of Christian practice and cultural habit cause a majority of people to have "Sundays off." This makes the first day of the week the most appropriate day for weekly Christian worship. But this must not be misunderstood as though there would be anything wrong with worship scheduled for other times. Therefore, many congregations have the practice of offering another weekly worship option, such as Saturday night or Monday night. This is in keeping with Christian freedom and the spirit of the Commandment to hallow the Sabbath day.

substance. The Greek term is "body" (see previous uses of the term at 1:22; 2:9, 11), which recalls Christ's incarnation. As a literal shadow is testimony of the literal body that casts it, so the OT practices mentioned here (and others like them) bear witness to the eternal Christ who established them and who fulfills them by His incarnation and ministry.

2:18 *disqualify.* This term can also have the meaning "cheat." The heretics were attempting to persuade the Colossian Christians that they could not be saved unless they adhered to the beliefs and practices of their group. Paul wrote to confirm his readers in the true faith lest the heretics turn them away from the truth and thereby "disqualify" them from salvation. *asceticism.* This word denotes false humility or abasement. From this verse we gather that the false teachers at Colossae advocated some form of religious asceticism as necessary for attaining a right standing with God. Melanchthon warned, "When people believe that they are pure and righteous because of such hypocrisy, they hinder the knowledge of Christ and the knowledge of God's gifts and commandments" (Ap XXIII 46). *worship of angels.* It is impossible to know exactly what this practice of the heretics involved. It seems all but certain that "angels" here is another term for what Paul called "elemental spirits" in 2:8 and 19 and for the various "powers" that he named in 1:16. Perhaps this "worship" involved actual acts of prayer and the like; since polytheism was very common in the Greco-Roman world, the worship of multiple beings would not have seemed out of place to many in that era. Whatever the particulars of this "worship of angels," it is evident that the heresy required some sort of inappropriate acknowledgement of these beings. *going on in detail about visions.* The heretics must have claimed special divine revelation as the source of their peculiar doctrines. Paul warned believers not to be deceived by those who claim special revelation. If it is not truly centered in Christ (v. 19), it is not of the Holy Spirit; rather, it comes from the sinful nature. This verse echoes the apostle's call for faithfulness in 1:23 and anticipates his directive to the Colossians to a worship life centered in the word of Christ (3:16). *sensuous mind.* The Greek has "mind of his flesh." "Flesh" was used with a variety of meanings by the apostle. The term can designate that which covers the bones (1Co 15:39) and by extension means the human body (Col 1:22, 24). "Flesh" can also be used, as here, to denote man's fallen, sinful nature (see also Rm 8:5–8; Col

2:11, 13, 18, 23). Paul set forth profound theological truths: (1) the material world is not inherently evil (it was created by God) and (2) mankind's rebellion against God has entirely corrupted his being. In the present passage Paul's meaning is clear: the heresy originates in sinful man and not in God.

2:19 *Head.* Christ is the Lord of all creation as well as the cause of our salvation (Eph 5:23). *growth.* All who are in Christ are growing, not because of their own self-imposed religious exercises, but because of the Word of Christ. This can be seen from a comparison of this passage with Eph 4:14–16 (see also 1:6; 3:16, and the notes there). Believers grow according to the growth God gives.

2:20–23 Regarding these verses, Melanchthon noted,

Paul says that traditions do not help with respect to eternal righteousness and eternal life, because food, drink, clothing, and the like are things that perish through use. Eternal life is worked in the heart by eternal things, that is, by God's Word and the Holy Spirit (Ap XXVIII 10).

2:20 *if with Christ you died.* They had died with Christ in Baptism (v. 12 and note). Hence, they were set free from any authority of the demonic spirits, so that there was no need to acknowledge them. *elemental spirits.* See the note at v. 8. *regulations.* Man-made regulations of false religion have nothing to do with Christ and the forgiveness of sins.

2:21 *handle . . . taste . . . touch.* Some interpreters have thought that these imperatives might be prohibitions by the false teachers against marriage and sexuality. However, the notation that these things "perish as they are used" (v. 22) effectively rules out that possibility. Those who seek salvation through their own efforts gravitate toward external exercises that are easily seen and measurable. Human efforts at salvation fall under the same verdict: they are false ways of salvation.

2:22 *perish as they are used.* The temporal nature of those things in which the Colossians were seeking their salvation points to the inability of these things to provide for eternal salvation. A religion constructed from decaying elements of this world is itself perishing. *human precepts.* See the note on "regulations" at v. 20. The wording here indicates that these precepts of men are set in opposition to the teachings of God.

2:23 *appearance of wisdom.* Human efforts at salvation seem right to fallen human reason. In reality, these have only an appearance of wisdom; they have no value before God. *self-made religion.* Self-imposed, external efforts (v. 21) are vital to those whose religion is more about them than it is about God. *no value.* Desires of the flesh cannot be overcome by self-denial. They can only be overcome by God's grace in Christ. The final phrase might be translated "they do not have any value but are for the gratification of the flesh," with the word "flesh" referring to humanity's fallen sinful nature. Manmade rules of asceticism—however severe and even heroic they may seem to human sight—may actually be a form of indulging one particular aspect of the "flesh"—that is, manmade practices like these may even be an indulgence of our sinful desire to save ourselves.

2:16–23 in Devotion and Prayer The Christian faith will not be replaced by man-made religion. Over the centuries, many have claimed to have found a substitute for Christ and His forgiveness: e.g., rationalism, socialism, and postmodernism. Sometimes these ideas are very impressive, and the lifestyles they conceive become extremely popular. But Paul wrote, "Let God be true though every one were a liar" (Rm 3:4). Waves of man-made wisdom and religion always end up breaking apart upon God's truth in Jesus, who "is the same yesterday and today and forever" (Heb 13:8). • Thank You, Lord, for granting me faith and preserving my faith with the wisdom and substance of Christ. Amen.

PART 2

PAUL'S INSTRUCTIONS (3:1–4:6)

The Christian Life (3:1–4:6)

Death and life (3:1–4)

ESV	KJV
3 ¹If then you have been raised with Christ, seek the things that are above, where Christ is, seated at the right hand of God. ²Set your minds on things that are above, not on things that are on earth. ³For you have died, and your life is hidden with Christ in God. ⁴When Christ who is your life appears, then you also will appear with him in glory.	3 ¹If ye then be risen with Christ, seek those things which are above, where Christ sitteth on the right hand of God. ²Set your affection on things above, not on things on the earth. ³For ye are dead, and your life is hid with Christ in God. ⁴When Christ, who is our life, shall appear, then shall ye also appear with him in glory.

Introduction to 3:1–17 Paul began here the practical section of his letter, which extends to 4:6. In this second portion of Colossians he instructed his readers in and exhorted them to godly living. His instruction and exhortation here is based on his teaching and proclamation in the first (doctrinal) portion of the letter (chs. 1–2), particularly what he had said there regarding Baptism.

3:1 *raised with Christ.* A comparison with 2:12 shows that a Christian's being raised with Christ took place in Baptism, which is a means to salvation and which enables him to live the Christian life. *things that are above.* These words are not to be understood spatially but theologically. In passages such as this, "above" designates those things that have to do with God (Jn 8:23). Hence, in their daily living, the Colossians were to seek those things that characterize their holy God. *right hand.* As throughout Scripture, God's "right hand" is not a place but a symbol of divine power (Ps 110; Mt 22:44). Our Lord's being seated at God's right hand means that He holds power and control over the entire universe. Gerhard wrote, "A highness not of place but of majesty is being described, and a loftiness of glory, something that is clear from opposition [of the spiritual and the carnal, vv. 2, 5]" (Gerhard E 4.221).

3:2 *on earth.* Paul did not despise the things of the earth (1Tm 4:4). However, in a passage like the present one, the term "earth" designated what is fallen, sinful, corrupt, and hence not pleasing to God (cf. Php 3:19). Such things God's people are to avoid.

3:3 *died.* This took place in their Baptism into Christ; see 2:20 and the note there. *hidden.* Here the word means something along the lines of "stored up for safe keeping" (compare its meaning in 2:3). In this world, our life with Christ and the accompanying blessings are often hidden under weakness and suffering. Our true life will be "revealed" (an alternate translation for "appear" in v. 4) at Christ's second coming. *in God.* On the meaning of this phrase, see the note at 1Th 1:1.

3:4 *you also will appear with Him in glory.* Our eternal life, which we possess now through Baptism, will be fully experienced at the resurrection. Through Christ, we are participants in God's glory (Jn 1:14; Php 3:21; see further the note on "hope of glory" at 1:27).

Put off and put on (3:5–17)

ESV	KJV
[5]Put to death therefore what is earthly in you: sexual immorality, impurity, passion, evil desire, and covetousness, which is idolatry. [6]On account of these the wrath of God is coming. [7]In these you too once walked, when you were living in them. [8]But now you must put them all away: anger, wrath, malice, slander, and obscene talk from your mouth.	[5]Mortify therefore your members which are upon the earth; fornication, uncleanness, inordinate affection, evil concupiscence, and covetousness, which is idolatry: [6]For which things' sake the wrath of God cometh on the children of disobedience: [7]In the which ye also walked some time, when ye lived in them. [8]But now ye also put off all these; anger, wrath, malice, blasphemy, filthy communication out of your mouth.

⁹Do not lie to one another, seeing that you have put off the old self with its practices ¹⁰and have put on the new self, which is being renewed in knowledge after the image of its creator. ¹¹Here there is not Greek and Jew, circumcised and uncircumcised, barbarian, Scythian, slave, free; but Christ is all, and in all. ¹²Put on then, as God's chosen ones, holy and beloved, compassionate hearts, kindness, humility, meekness, and patience, ¹³bearing with one another and, if one has a complaint against another, forgiving each other; as the Lord has forgiven you, so you also must forgive. ¹⁴And above all these put on love, which binds everything together in perfect harmony. ¹⁵And let the peace of Christ rule in your hearts, to which indeed you were called in one body. And be thankful. ¹⁶Let the word of Christ dwell in you richly, teaching and admonishing one another in all wisdom, singing psalms and hymns and spiritual songs, with thankfulness in your hearts to God. ¹⁷And whatever you do, in word or deed, do everything in the name of the Lord Jesus, giving thanks to God the Father through him.

⁹Lie not one to another, seeing that ye have put off the old man with his deeds; ¹⁰And have put on the new man, which is renewed in knowledge after the image of him that created him: ¹¹Where there is neither Greek nor Jew, circumcision nor uncircumcision, Barbarian, Scythian, bond nor free: but Christ is all, and in all. ¹²Put on therefore, as the elect of God, holy and beloved, bowels of mercies, kindness, humbleness of mind, meekness, longsuffering; ¹³Forbearing one another, and forgiving one another, if any man have a quarrel against any: even as Christ forgave you, so also do ye. ¹⁴And above all these things put on charity, which is the bond of perfectness. ¹⁵And let the peace of God rule in your hearts, to the which also ye are called in one body; and be ye thankful. ¹⁶Let the word of Christ dwell in you richly in all wisdom; teaching and admonishing one another in psalms and hymns and spiritual songs, singing with grace in your hearts to the Lord. ¹⁷And whatsoever ye do in word or deed, do all in the name of the Lord Jesus, giving thanks to God and the Father by him.

3:5 *Put to death*. Christians died with Christ (2:20; 3:3) in Baptism (2:12). On the basis of that which Christ has already done for them and their salvation, Paul called Christians to live out their death with Christ by renouncing sin. He continued by listing examples of sins to be renounced. *covetousness, which is idolatry*. The apostle styled covetousness as idolatry, because covetousness makes what is desired into a god. Luther warned, "Whatever you set your heart on and put your trust in is truly your god" (LC I 3; cf. Mt 6:24).

3:6 *wrath of God is coming.* God's attitude toward sin (Rm 1:18) and unbelief (Jn 3:36) will be fully revealed in the final judgment. The phrase "on the children of disobedience" appears in most early Greek manuscripts for Colossians but is missing in a few of the very earliest, making scholars wonder whether it was part of the original Letter. The very same phrase occurs in Eph 5:6 and it may be that scribes dropped it from Colossians or added it from their memory of Ephesians as sometimes happens with familiar, similar passages.

3:8 *put them all away.* The Greek is actually "put off" (so KJV), as a person might "put off" dirty clothing. The practice of post-NT times (which may well have existed already in NT times) was in keeping with this kind of language about Baptism. The candidate removed old clothing for Baptism, after which he was clad in a new, clean garment. Such language and the corresponding practices present Baptism as a divine way of cleansing from sins and consequently of empowering the baptized for new living. This imagery harkens back to passages such as Is 52:1; 61:10; Zec 3:1–5.

3:9 *old self.* A literal translation is "old man" (so KJV). The contrast between the "old man" and "new man" (a literal translation of the term in 3:10) is common in Christian writings. The old man/old self is the sinful corruption of our nature inherited from Adam (see the following note).

3:10 *new self.* In Baptism, we put on Christ (Gal 3:27) and enter into a saving relationship with Him. Hence, just as the "old man" is our sinful nature inherited from Adam, so the "new man" is our right standing before God that is ours because of our saving relationship with Christ, the second or last Adam (1Co 15:45–47). *image of its creator.* Our new relationship of faith restores the image of God that was lost because of sin. The image consists in knowledge of God and holiness. Therefore, the restoration of the divine image means the restoration of a right relationship with God. The restoration of God's image also bestows power for a new, godly way of living. Nevertheless, the full realization of the effects of the restoration of the divine image awaits the resurrection and the life to come (Rm 8:29; 1Co 15:49; Php 3:21). See further the note at 1:15. Melanchthon observed,

> The image of God is the knowledge of God, righteousness, and truth. [Peter] Lombard is not afraid to say that original righteousness "is the very likeness to God which God implanted in man" (Ap II 20–21).

3:11 In Christ, distinctions are removed, whether national (Greek and Jew), social (barbarian and Scythian), or economic (slave and free). *Scythian.* This term denotes people from present-day southern Russia. The Greeks thought them to be the most barbaric of the barbarians. *all, and in all.* This expression denotes that the created order has been restored to what it ought to be. Although this has already been inaugurated for this age (Eph 1:21, 23), it will be consummated in the age to come (Eph 1:21; 1Co 15:28).

3:12 *put on.* See the notes at vv. 8, 10. Virtues such as these are not ours to accomplish but are gifts God provided. They are Christ's virtues. *chosen ones.* Israel was so designated in the OT (Dt 4:37). The church (believers in Christ) is the "new Israel," the new people of God (cf. 1Pt 2:9). *holy.* See the note at 1:2. *humility.* The virtue of "humility" involves displaying the mind of Christ, which a believer has when he is "in Christ" (Php 2:3–4 in light of vv. 5–11; on the phrase "in Christ" and expressions equivalent to it, see the note at 1:2). *meekness.* Another translation would be "gentleness." Although the rendering "meekness" may perhaps conjure up notions of weakness, the Christian virtue of gentleness is a virtue of strength. It is the strength to deal gently with another so as to be of help rather than hurting or offending (Gal 6:1; 2Tm 2:25). As a strong man can set a heavy object so gently on a fragile surface that it will not damage it, so the Christian has the strength of gentleness to deal with others without hurting them. *patience.* An alternate translation would be "longsuffering." This virtue means bearing with others in spite of their failings and doing so not just for a little while but, as we say, "for the long haul."

3:13 *bearing with one another.* As we each struggle with our own temptations, so we understand the struggles of others. *you also must forgive.* Luther echoed this while explaining the Fifth Petition of the Lord's Prayer (Mt 6:12). Forgiving others shows that we truly believe God has forgiven us.

3:14 *love.* See 1Co 13:13. *harmony.* The KJV wording, "the bond of perfection," may better serve the larger context. In light of the language of putting off and on in these verses, the picture seems to be of love acting like a belt, which holds all these virtues together.

3:15 *rule.* The peace of Christ acts as a judge or umpire to decide disputes within the Christian community. *and be thankful.* Note how the virtues of the Christian life that Paul mentioned in these verses are relational, that is, they cannot be practiced in isolation but must be carried out through interacting with others. The exhortation to be thankful is no exception to this, for a Christian's thanksgiving is offered not only for himself but for others. Paul himself was a good example of offering such thanksgiving for the blessings received by others (e.g., Col 1:3).

3:16 *Let the word of Christ dwell.* Since the Word of God is the means to eternal blessing (see 1:25–28), the apostle directed his readers to Christ's Word for their own spiritual good. *in you.* The Greek for "you" here is plural (as are the participles "teaching," "admonishing," and "singing"); hence, "among you" would also be an acceptable translation. Although Paul's instruction here has application to any use of the Word of God, in view of all these plurals, his words have special relevance to the **corporate** worship of God's people as they are gathered around Word and Sacrament (that is, in the divine service). *richly.* Related to the word "riches" in 1:27, this term here means not only "a great deal" but also "with great benefit." *singing psalms and hymns and spiritual songs.* These terms include OT psalms as well as NT hymns (1:15–20; Eph 5:14; Php 2:6–11; 1Tm 3:16; see also the poetic portions of Luke 1 and 2). A comparison of this verse with its companion passage in Eph 5:19 makes it very clear that Christian music includes not only hymns addressed to God but also those that are a vehicle to speak the Word of God to others. Songs conveyed some of the Bible's greatest teachings. Great expressions of joy and thankfulness naturally flow from the rich doctrine of Christ. *with thankfulness.* The KJV provides a time honored way of translating this Greek expression as "with grace." The Greek term for grace often occurs in expressions for thanks (cf. the similar usage in modern Spanish where one says "Thank you" with "Gracias," related to the term for grace).

This verse and the parallel in Eph 5:19–20 also present both the sacramental dimension of worship (God bestows His salvation on us in His Word and Sacraments) and its sacrificial dimension (we respond with prayer, praise, and a life of service to Him). Thus, the Word of God that is both spoken and sung will be the central focus of Christian worship. (See the note at 4:16 on the reading of God's Word in worship.) Luther wrote,

> Certainly you will not release a stronger incense or other repellant against the devil than to be engaged by God's commandments and words, and speak, sing, or think them (LC Longer Preface 10).

3:17 *everything.* There is no division between the sacred and the secular concerning what a Christian says and does to the glory of God. Christ should accompany us in all facets of life. *giving thanks.* The importance of thanksgiving may be seen in that Paul has mentioned it three times in the space of three verses!

3:1–17 in Devotion and Prayer What is the good life? Prosperity, popularity, pleasure? No, it is the life we receive from Jesus, including gifts that we cannot make or purchase: forgiveness, love, peace, and thankfulness. Jesus' life fills us with virtues rather than vices and enables us to be a blessing rather than a bane to others.
• "Before the dawning day Let sin's dark deeds be gone, The sinful self be put away, The new self now put on." Amen. (*LSB* 331:5)

Table of duties (3:18–4:1)

ESV	KJV
[18]Wives, submit to your husbands, as is fitting in the Lord. [19]Husbands, love your wives, and do not be harsh with them. [20]Children, obey your parents in everything, for this pleases the Lord. [21]Fathers, do not provoke your children, lest they become discouraged. [22]Slaves, obey in everything those who are your earthly masters, not by way of eye-service, as people-pleasers, but with sincerity of heart, fearing the Lord. [23]Whatever you do, work heartily, as for the Lord and not for men, [24]knowing that from the Lord you will receive the inheritance as your reward. You are serving the Lord Christ. [25]For the wrongdoer will be paid back for the wrong he has done, and there is no partiality. 4 [1]Masters, treat your slaves justly and fairly, knowing that you also have a Master in heaven.	[18]Wives, submit yourselves unto your own husbands, as it is fit in the Lord. [19]Husbands, love your wives, and be not bitter against them. [20]Children, obey your parents in all things: for this is well pleasing unto the Lord. [21]Fathers, provoke not your children to anger, lest they be discouraged. [22]Servants, obey in all things your masters according to the flesh; not with eyeservice, as menpleasers; but in singleness of heart, fearing God; [23]And whatsoever ye do, do it heartily, as to the Lord, and not unto men; [24]Knowing that of the Lord ye shall receive the reward of the inheritance: for ye serve the Lord Christ. [25]But he that doeth wrong shall receive for the wrong which he hath done: and there is no respect of persons. 4 [1]Masters, give unto your servants that which is just and equal; knowing that ye also have a Master in heaven.

Introduction to 3:18–4:1 In this section, Paul applied to our various vocations the general principles of Christ-centered living discussed above. An individual Christian may have a number of such vocations in life: husband or wife, parent or child, employer or employee (compare this section with Eph 5:21–6:9 and 1Pt 2:13–3:7; this latter passage includes instruction regarding the vocations we might term *governors* and *governed*).

3:18 *submit*. This term, which one can also translate as "be subject," means being in one's proper, orderly arrangement toward others. There is nothing demeaning about this word: as a boy, Jesus submitted to His parents (Lk 2:51), and in eternity the risen and exalted Christ will be subject to the heavenly Father (1Co 15:28). Working together in harmony necessitates that one leads and another follows, much like members of an athletic team do to achieve a united success.

3:19 *love*. Husbands must lead the way in love, just as Jesus leads the way in His love for us (cf. Eph 5:25).

3:20 *Children*. This letter was to be read in public worship (see 4:16 and note). By speaking directly to children, Paul pointed out that children were considered members of the Church and part of worship. This was a noteworthy departure from the common attitude toward children at that time. *everything*. Children are to obey unless directed to do something sinful (Ac 5:29).

3:21 *provoke*. Literally, "embitter." Discipline and encouragement, Law and Gospel, are necessary when raising children. The imperative is addressed especially to fathers, not because it is inapplicable to mothers but to emphasize the leading role that fathers are to take in the nurture of children.

3:22 *Slaves*. There were significant differences between the institution of slavery in the NT world and those found in other eras of history (with all of their accompanying abuses). In the Roman Empire it was in the interest of masters to offer fair treatment and the prospect of eventual freedom to keep their slaves willing to work. Furthermore, slaves also performed "white collar" professions, such as artisans, teachers, and doctors. Moreover, race played a minimal (if any) role in Roman slavery (see also Ex 21:2–6; Dt 15:12–17). Thus, biblical directives to masters and slaves are largely applicable to modern employer/employee relationships or to lender/debtor relationships (if you are not convinced that borrowing money is akin to slavery, stop making payments and see what happens!). The Scriptures neither condone slavery and its potential abuses nor advocate violent overthrow of social order. Onesimus, a slave, assisted in delivering this Letter to the Colossians (4:9). He and Tychicus also delivered a Letter to Onesimus's master, Philemon, who lived in Colossae. Christianity eventually emerged as the dominant influence in Western culture. As a result, society in large measure did away with the institution of human slavery (cf. Schmidt, *How Christianity Changed the World*). Christianity did this by (1) treating slaves as equals in the churches (1Co 7:20–24); (2) reminding masters that they too had a Master (Col 4:1); (3) treating slaves as persons with both rights and responsibilities (Col 3:22–25); (4) asserting the dignity of manual labor (Eph 4:28); and (5) pointing to the example of Christ as one who suffered unjustly (1Pt 2:21). *earthly masters.* The literal rendering of the KJV ("according to the flesh") allows the reader to see the various parallel references to "the flesh" that occur in the doctrinal portions of the letter (chs. 1–2). *eye-service.* Service rendered merely for those who are looking.

3:23 *heartily.* A more literal translation would be "from the soul." We are to work from our true, inner being.

3:24 *inheritance.* The use of this term to refer to our eternal salvation emphasizes that it is a gift of grace (one does not earn or work for an inheritance as he does for a paycheck). Whatever unfairness we may experience on earth is nothing compared to the splendor of our inheritance in Christ (1:12).

3:25 *no partiality.* That God judges justly and shows no favoritism is a warning to all—and a word of encouragement to those who are suffering unjustly (Jn 5:30).

4:1 *Master in heaven.* The treatment that a leader gives to someone subject to him is affected by his relationship to the Lord who has redeemed him and to whom he owes allegiance. Note the play on words in this verse: "masters" and "Master" (the Greek term is ordinarily translated "Lord" when referring, as here, to God/Christ).

3:18–4:1 in Devotion and Prayer People live in interrelationships with one another. These include the realms of marriage and the family as well as that of economic systems. The heart of our old nature wishes to seek personal advantage, which causes frustration, resentment, and violence in relationships. Paul urged us to resist this temptation, no matter what our calling in life may be. Faithful resistance becomes a reality when we live by faith "in the Son of God, who loved [us] and gave Himself for [us]" (Gal 2:20). In Christ, we know that we will not miss out on anything. • Lord, You created us for righteous relationships and work, not to harm others by lording our authority over them. Lead us to spend our lives in loving service for You and for others, for You have so dearly loved us. Amen.

Watch and pray (4:2–6)

ESV	KJV
[2]Continue steadfastly in prayer, being watchful in it with thanksgiving. [3]At the same time, pray also for us, that God may open to us a door for the word, to declare the mystery of Christ, on account of which I am in prison—[4]that I may make it clear, which is how I ought to speak. [5]Walk in wisdom toward outsiders, making the best use of the time. [6]Let your speech always be gracious, seasoned with salt, so that you may know how you ought to answer each person.	[2]Continue in prayer, and watch in the same with thanksgiving; [3]Withal praying also for us, that God would open unto us a door of utterance, to speak the mystery of Christ, for which I am also in bonds: [4]That I may make it manifest, as I ought to speak. [5]Walk in wisdom toward them that are without, redeeming the time. Let your speech be always with grace, seasoned with salt, that ye may know how ye ought to answer every man.

Introduction to 4:2–6 Paul concluded his exhortations regarding the Christian's new life of sanctified living with some more general directives regarding Christian conduct. He focused on our life of prayer and on using all our speech with care.

4:2 *continue steadfastly in prayer.* The Letter began with Paul's emphasis on prayer (1:3, 9). Therefore, his words regarding prayer there and here serve as thematic "bookends" to his Letter. For a similar literary device in Colossians, see the note on "grace" at 4:18. Paul wrapped up and supported all his doctrine and exhortation with devoted prayers for God's blessings.

4:3 *pray also for us.* Calvin wrote,

He does not say this by way of pretence, but because, being conscious to himself of his own necessity, he was earnestly desirous to be aided by their prayers, and was fully persuaded that they would be of advantage to them. Who then, in the present day, would dare to despise the intercessions of brethren, which Paul openly declares himself to stand in need of? And, unquestionably, it is not in vain that the Lord has appointed this exercise of love between us—that we pray for each other. Not only, therefore, ought each of us to pray for his brethren, but we ought also, on our part, diligently to seek help from the prayers of others, as often as occasion requires. (Calvin 223).

open to us a door. A comparison with the similar request of Eph 6:19–20 suggests that the apostle's longing here is not only that God would provide opportunities to speak His saving Word but also that He would give him the courage to take advantage of these opportunities (see also 1Co 16:9). *mystery.* See the note at 1:27. *prison.* In 2Co 11:23, Paul spoke of frequent imprisonments. These were an aspect of his "suffering with Christ" (Rm 8:17). See pp. 62–63. Verses 2 and 3 suggest that the apostle had at least a reasonable expectation at this point that he would be freed from the current imprisonment. We know from his subsequent letters to Timothy and Titus that this indeed was the case (1Tm 1:3; 2Tm 4:20; Ti 1:5; 3:12; see also Rm 15:24, 28; Php 2:23–24; Phm 22).

4:4 *make it clear.* This could also be translated "make it manifest" or "make it known." The Law is already made plain by creation (Rm 1:18–20) and conscience (Rm 2:14–16), but the Gospel is only made known through the proclamation about Christ (Rm 3:21–26). We clarify the mystery of the Gospel by simply presenting it in its purity so that all people can understand it.

4:5 *wisdom.* On this word, see the note at 1:9. In the next verse Paul applied this general directive about wisdom to the particular instance of the use of our speech. *outsiders.* Our life before unbelievers should put a favorable light on the Word we proclaim (Jas 3:13).

4:6 *graciousness.* This Greek word is often translated "grace" (hence the KJV translation). While the apostle's exhortation certainly pertains to our speaking the grace of God by speaking the Gospel, his words apply to all our speech. Our words should be as appealing as properly seasoned food (hence, the statement that follows). *seasoned with salt.* We should strive for sincerity, tact, and eloquence so that our conversational style is always tasteful. For a good example, see Paul's Letter to Philemon. On the other hand vulgarity, gossip, and pretentiousness are some of the things that demean our speech and hence can even undermine our witness.

4:2–6 in Devotion and Prayer All of our speech, but especially our prayer and our proclamation, is to be used to God's glory and in keeping with His will. • "Keep me from saying words That later need recalling; Guard me lest idle speech May from my lips be falling; But when within my place I must and ought to speak, Then to my words give grace Lest I offend the weak." Amen. (*LSB* 696:3; TPH 277)

The Prison Epistles and Persecution

The Prison Epistles of Paul remind us of the persecution that Paul and many early Christians suffered for the Gospel. In many parts of the modern world, Christians continue to suffer for their faith. This is to be expected, but God furnishes strength and endurance, and we continue to pray for our brothers and sisters in the faith.

During the apostle Paul's missionary journeys, Jews in various places resisted the Gospel message. On occasion, this resistance became violent. (See Paul's list of hardships at 2Co 11:23–33.)

This smoldering Jewish resentment was fanned into flames when Paul returned to Jerusalem after his third missionary journey and appeared in the temple. There, a group of Asian Jews incited a riot by publicly accusing Paul of forsaking the Law of Moses and polluting the temple by bringing a Gentile into the area reserved exclusively for Jews. The charges were false, but even so, they aroused the anti-Christian element in Jerusalem. Paul would doubtless have been stoned to death on the spot had not the Roman garrison commander intervened and brought a detachment of soldiers to stem the fury of the mob (Ac 21:27–36).

When an attempt by the apostle to defend himself before his Jewish accusers resulted in another near riot, the commander detained Paul (Ac 22). Hoping to have the charges against the apostle clarified, he called an informal meeting of the Jewish Council (Sanhedrin), but that meeting also degenerated into a shouting match. Meanwhile, Paul assured humane treatment for himself by informing the commander that he was a Roman citizen. When a plot on Paul's life was discovered, the commander had Paul removed to the seat of the imperial government at Caesarea (Ac 23).

With his arrival at Caesarea, Paul began an almost five-year period of unjust and unwarranted captivity, hearings, and appeals. After several years of imprisonment in Caesarea, Paul was convinced that he would never receive a fair trial in either Jerusalem or Caesarea. So he exercised his right as a Roman citizen to appeal his case directly to the emperor in Rome. Festus, the Roman governor in Palestine at that time, somewhat unwillingly granted Paul his appeal. Ac 27–28 describe Paul's long and perilous journey to Rome.

At Rome, the appeal process dragged on for more than two years. During this time, though constantly chained to a guard, Paul was able to receive friends and continue his ministry.

We do not know why Paul's hearing was delayed so long in Rome. In his Epistle to the Philippians, which is considered the last of the four Prison Epistles—the others being Ephesians, Colossians, and Philemon—Paul informed the Philippians that his first hearing had taken place and that it had gone well. Though he did not foolishly ignore the possibility that the emperor might still rule against him, Paul was optimistic that he would be acquitted and set free.

Based on what Paul says in Philippians and the Pastoral Epistles, he was likely set free from this first Roman imprisonment (AD 58–60) and continued to work until he was imprisoned again in the general persecution of Christians that took place under Emperor Nero in AD 67. During this second imprisonment, Paul wrote 2 Timothy, the last testimony of a Christian man facing his earthly end. ❧

PART 3

CONCLUSION (4:7–18)

Concluding Matters (4:7–18)

ESV	KJV
⁷Tychicus will tell you all about my activities. He is a beloved brother and faithful minister and fellow servant in the Lord. ⁸I have sent him to you for this very purpose, that you may know how we are and that he may encourage your hearts, ⁹and with him Onesimus, our faithful and beloved brother, who is one of you. They will tell you of everything that has taken place here.	⁷All my state shall Tychicus declare unto you, who is a beloved brother, and a faithful minister and fellowservant in the Lord: ⁸Whom I have sent unto you for the same purpose, that he might know your estate, and comfort your hearts; ⁹With Onesimus, a faithful and beloved brother, who is one of you. They shall make known unto you all things which are done here.
¹⁰Aristarchus my fellow prisoner greets you, and Mark the cousin of Barnabas (concerning whom you have received instructions—if he comes to you, welcome him), ¹¹and Jesus who is called Justus. These are the only men of the circumcision among my fellow workers for the kingdom of God, and they have been a comfort to me. ¹²Epaphras, who is one of you, a servant of Christ Jesus, greets you, always struggling on your behalf in his prayers, that you may stand mature and fully assured in all the will of God. ¹³For I bear him witness that he has worked hard for you and for those in Laodicea and in Hierapolis. ¹⁴Luke the beloved physician greets you, as does Demas.	¹⁰Aristarchus my fellowprisoner saluteth you, and Marcus, sister's son to Barnabas, (touching whom ye received commandments: if he come unto you, receive him;) ¹¹And Jesus, which is called Justus, who are of the circumcision. These only are my fellowworkers unto the kingdom of God, which have been a comfort unto me. ¹²Epaphras, who is one of you, a servant of Christ, saluteth you, always labouring fervently for you in prayers, that ye may stand perfect and complete in all the will of God. ¹³For I bear him record, that he hath a great zeal for you, and them that are in Laodicea, and them in Hierapolis. ¹⁴Luke, the beloved physician, and Demas, greet you.

¹⁵Give my greetings to the brothers at Laodicea, and to Nympha and the church in her house. ¹⁶And when this letter has been read among you, have it also read in the church of the Laodiceans; and see that you also read the letter from Laodicea. ¹⁷And say to Archippus, "See that you fulfill the ministry that you have received in the Lord."

¹⁸I, Paul, write this greeting with my own hand. Remember my chains. Grace be with you.

¹⁵Salute the brethren which are in Laodicea, and Nymphas, and the church which is in his house.

¹⁶And when this epistle is read among you, cause that it be read also in the church of the Laodiceans; and that ye likewise read the epistle from Laodicea.

¹⁷And say to Archippus, Take heed to the ministry which thou hast received in the Lord, that thou fulfil it.

¹⁸The salutation by the hand of me Paul. Remember my bonds. Grace be with you. Amen.

Introduction to 4:7–18 The concluding sections of Paul's Letters (some of which are rather lengthy) may include such things as his plans for the future, greetings, commendations, and blessings. The greetings in Colossians are far longer than in any other Pauline Letters except for Romans. These are the only two Letters of the apostle written to churches that he had not personally visited. Such greetings, extended to those whom Paul knew personally and to the addressees of the letter, served to establish common ties between Paul and his readers.

4:7 *Tychicus.* A comparison with Eph 6:21 points to Col and Eph both being carried by Tychicus and, therefore, almost certainly at the same time. On the writing of Colossians and Ephesians, see the note at 4:16. Tychicus was a valued coworker of Paul, who sent him as his representative to places where he himself could not be (2Tm 4:12; Ti 3:12).

4:8 Good ministry begins when we listen first to the people we serve and when we apply the appropriate Word of God to bring encouragement in the faith. On "encourage," see the note at 1Th 4:18.

4:9 *Onesimus.* This man was a runaway slave from Colossae who came to Paul and was converted. Although Onesimus became a faithful Christian, Paul did not describe him as a Gospel worker because his availability for that service was still to be determined by Philemon, his master. See the Letter to Philemon.

4:10 *Aristarchus.* Paul's colleague from Thessalonica accompanied him to Ephesus, to Jerusalem, and to Rome. He was probably with Paul while he was under house arrest and attended to his needs (Ac 19:29; 20:4; 27:2). *fellow prisoner.* This Greek term could also be rendered "my fellow prisoner of war." Paul's military language suggests that he viewed his ministry as a battle against evil (cf. Php 2:25). *Mark . . . Barnabas.* Mark's full name was John Mark. That he was a cousin to Barnabas may, at least in part, explain why Barnabas supported Mark during the second missionary journey when Paul and Barnabas disputed over Mark's service and decided to go on separate missionary journeys (Ac 15:37–40). It is encouraging to know that Paul and Mark (and hence also Paul and Barnabas) were later reconciled (see also 2Tm 4:11).

4:11 *Jesus who is called Justus.* This disciple is mentioned only here in the NT. "Jesus" ("Jeshua" in Aramaic) was a common Jewish name of the time. *men of the circumcision.* This is another way of referring to those who were Jews. Epaphras, Luke, and Demas (vv. 12–14) were Gentiles. *comfort.* This renders a Greek word that occurs only here in the NT; it is not the same word that is translated "encourage" in v. 8, a word that is sometimes translated "comfort." On the term "encourage" see the notes at 2Th 2:16 and especially 1Th 4:18. The word used here refers to such things as companionship and emotional solace. Although these benefits are not on a par with the comfort/encouragement given by God the Holy Spirit, they are still important blessings that God's people provide to others.

4:12 *Epaphras.* He was most likely the founding pastor of the Church at Colossae (cf. 1:7 and the note there). *one of you.* This means that Epaphras was a Colossian. *struggling . . . in his prayers.* His intercessory prayers are conspicuous and commendable. Prayer is not always relaxing or meditative, as the Psalms attest. *mature.* The focus of his prayers indicated the overall message to the Colossians—that they would remain steadfast and grow to maturity in their faith in Christ.

4:13 *Laodicea . . . Hierapolis.* Paul's concern extended to others in the Lycus Valley. It seems that Epaphras served as pastor in all three of these three churches. Paul's pastoral concern for the believers in these cities suggests that he was supervising the ministry there as part of his work of supervising ministry throughout the Roman province of Asia (that seems to be the implication of Ac 19:10).

4:14 *Luke.* Only here is Luke described as a physician, but there are indications of his medical background in his writings (e.g., Lk 22:44; Ac 28:8). Early tradition holds that he was a physician from Antioch in Syria (e.g., *NPNF*2 1:136). *Demas.* He later turned away from the faith (2Tm 4:10). As our Lord had his Judas, and Paul had his Demas, so pastors and other Christians in other times and places may also experience the heartache of a dear companion who falls from the faith.

4:15 *Nympha . . . church in her house.* Some texts read "his house" (e.g., KJV). The name Nympha can be either feminine or masculine. There is no way to be certain of gender, but we can be certain of this person's generosity and support for the Gospel. Paul himself would often begin Christian work in a city in the local Jewish synagogue (Ac 17:2), but he was almost always forced by opponents to move his new congregation and to continue his work elsewhere. Without their own houses of worship, the earliest Christians often met in homes for worship, as recounted, for example, in Ac 2:46 and 18:7 (see Ac 19:9 for an instance when the apostle made other arrangements).

4:16 *read among you.* The term used here suggests public, oral reading, as one would read the Holy Scriptures (Lk 4:16; Ac 13:27; cf. 1Tm 4:13). With this statement Paul placed his own Letters and teaching on par with the OT Scriptures (see 1Th 5:27; cf. also 1Co 15:37; Php 4:9; 2Th 2:15; 2Tm 1:13; 2:2; 3:14 [in light of 15–17]). Early Jewish and Christian teachers commonly sent out circular letters that would be read at a variety of places. *the letter from Laodicea.* In view of the status that Paul accorded this Letter (to be read publicly as the present Letter was to be read) this must have been one of his other Letters. It is quite likely that this Letter was the general Letter that we now know as Ephesians (some important Greek manuscripts of Ephesians omit the phrase "in Ephesus" from Eph 1:1, suggesting that this Letter was sent to a number of congregations, with the name of the city of address being inserted at the appropriate point in the greeting of the Letter). The carrying of both Colossians and Ephesians by Tychicus (see note at 4:7) also supports the identification of "the Letter from Laodicea" with Ephesians.

4:17 *Archippus.* He is called Paul's "fellow soldier" in Phm 2 (see the note on "my fellow prisoner" at 4:10). Some think he was Philemon's son. *ministry that you have received in the Lord.* We cannot be sure of the nature of this ministry. (The suggestion that the Letter to Philemon is actually addressed mainly to Archippus and that the ministry he received was to release Onesimus for service alongside the apostle, is highly tenuous at best.) Paul's encouragement demonstrates that ministry belongs not to us but to Christ, who distributes gifts of service and callings.

4:18 *my own hand.* In antiquity a secretary was customarily used for the actual penning of most letters (cf. Rm 16:22). Paul would take the pen in his own hand and write a bit at the end of his Letters. This served as his mark of authenticity (cf. 1Co 16:21; Gal 6:11; 2Th 3:17; Phm 19). Evidently there was something distinctive about his handwriting, such as large letters. This mark of authenticity (and hence apostolic authority) served to buttress his commendation of this Letter as being on a par with the OT Scriptures (see note at 4:16). *my chains.* Along with 4:3, 10, this verse points to the apostle being in prison at the writing of this letter. Imprisonment was one of the many things that he suffered for the sake of Christ (see further the note at 1:24; also pp. 62–63). Although Paul often expressed hope and joy in the face of persecution, he always needed and desired the prayers and encouragement of his fellow believers. *Grace.* Paul used this significant word near both the beginning (e.g., Col 1:2, 6) and the end of all his Letters. The apostle's "opening and closing remarks" have to do with grace, for God's undeserved favor for the sake of Christ is the believers' constant refuge, now and forever. In the KJV translation, "Amen" is at the end of the Letter as found in most Greek manuscripts. The appearance of this liturgical term may reflect the early Christian practice of publicly reading the apostle's Letter as part of the regular worship service.

4:2–18 in Devotion and Prayer Until this concluding section of Colossians, Paul had presented to his readers (and to us) a beautiful explanation of Christ's person and work. We do not need to turn to ourselves, to angels, or to anything else. Jesus is our true God and Savior. The "grocery list" of concluding instructions in 4:7–18 shows that the Gospel is not an abstract idea. It is the essential truth that transforms individual lives, such as those mentioned here, and continues to transform one person after another. • Dear Father, thank You for the individuals You use to proclaim to me the Gospel of forgiveness in Christ. Continue to use me to bring that saving message to my relatives, friends, and acquaintances. Give me boldness in sharing with them the blessings I have learned in studying Paul's Letter to the Colossians. Amen.

1 THESSALONIANS

INTRODUCTION TO
1 THESSALONIANS

Overview

Author

Paul the apostle

Date

c. AD 51

Places

Thessalonica; Macedonia; Achaia; Philippi; Athens

People

Paul; Silvanus; Timothy; Thessalonian Church; persecutors

Purpose

To restore relations with the Thessalonian Christians after persecution

separated Paul and his colleagues from the congregation

Law and Sin Themes

Imitation; affliction; parental care; God's Word at work; God's wrath; sanctification; idleness

Grace and Gospel Themes

The Gospel message; deliverance; God's Word at work; established blameless; resurrection of the dead; salvation; complete sanctification; God's faithfulness

Memory Verses

The resurrection of the dead (4:16–18); blameless in Christ (5:23–24)

Luther on 1 Thessalonians

St. Paul writes out of especial love and apostolic solicitude. For in the first two chapters he praises them because they received the gospel from him with such earnestness that they remained steadfast in it despite suffering and persecution, and became a beautiful example of faith to all congregations everywhere, and suffered persecution from their own kinsfolk like Christ and his apostles did from the Jews—as St. Paul by way of example had himself also suffered and led a holy life when he was with them. For this he thanks God, that his gospel had borne such fruit among them.

In chapter 3 he shows his care and solicitude that this labor of his and their praiseworthy beginning not be brought to nothing by the devil and his apostles through the doctrines of men. For this reason he sent Timothy to them beforehand to make sure about this. And he thanks God that things were still right among them and hopes that they continue to increase.

In chapter 4 he exhorts them to guard against sin and to do good to one another. He also answers a question which they had presented to him through Timothy concerning the resurrection of the dead, whether all would rise at once, or whether some after others.

In chapter 5 he writes of the Last Day, how it shall come suddenly and quickly. He gives them some good directions for governing other people and tells them what attitude they are to take toward the lives and teachings of others. (LW 35:386–87)

Calvin on 1 Thessalonians

The greater part of this Epistle consists of exhortations. Paul had instructed the Thessalonians in the right faith. On hearing, however, that persecutions were raging there, he had sent Timothy with the view of animating them for the conflict, that they might not give way through fear, as human infirmity is apt to do. Having been afterwards informed by Timothy respecting their entire condition, he employs various arguments to confirm them in steadfastness of faith, as well as in patience, should they be called to endure anything for the testimony of the gospel. (Calvin 235)

Gerhard on 1 Thessalonians

Thessalonica was a town at the mouth of the Macedonian Bay, located at the middle of a bend in the coast. There the apostle, through his preaching of the Gospel, had converted some Jews and Gentiles to Christ (Acts 17:2). However, because of persecution that the still-unbelieving Jews had stirred up against him, he was not able to remain there long. When he realized that the church he had recently planted was falling into great danger because it was afraid of persecutions, he sent Timothy to it to strengthen the Thessalonians in their faith. Timothy noticed that they were not at all terrified by persecutions, that they were still constant in their faith and patient in their adversities, and he related everything to the apostle faithfully. So, in this Epistle, Paul praises them and bears witness to their faithfulness, care, and concern on their behalf. (Gerhard E 1.264)

Challenges for Readers

Paul's Authorship. Some critics argue that 1 Thessalonians is composed of fragments from Paul's genuine Letters. In particular, they regard 2:14–16 as a later insertion because it refers to persecution of Christians in Judea. Note that, although the passage does refer to persecution in Judea, it describes the events of Ac 17:5–13. With this in view, there is no reason to regard the passage as an insertion.

Intermediate State. An important description for understanding the state of believers after death and before the resurrection of the body is given in 4:13–15. Here, Paul refers to the state of death as sleep, a common expression for death that does not imply the doctrine of "soul sleep" (unconsciousness). The dead in Christ enjoy the rest, comfort, and bliss of God's presence, though they will experience the fullness of eternal life only after the resurrection of their bodies on the Last Day.

The "Rapture" Doctrine. Some evangelicals regard 4:17 as a description of a secret return of Christ, which will take place before Christ's second coming in judgment (see note, 4:17). The passage actually describes the manner of Christ's return in judgment, when He will raise the dead (Mt 25:31–46; Jn 5:28–29; Ac 24:15; 1Th 4:13–15; Rv 1:7; 20:11–15). The events accord with the Apostles' Creed's order and summary, "He will come to judge the living and the dead. I believe in . . . the resurrection of the body, and the life everlasting."

Blessings for Readers

The value of the exhortation section of 1 Thessalonians may be measured by the fact that these two brief chapters have furnished no less than three Epistle readings in the ancient church's lectionary system: the Epistle for the second Sunday in Lent (1Th 4:1–7), and for the twenty-fifth and twenty-seventh Sundays after Trinity (1Th 4:13–18; 5:1–11).

Few letters offer more sustenance for the hope of God's people than this one. Besides the two great sections on the lot of the dead in Christ (4:13–18) and on the times and seasons of the Lord's return (5:1–11), note the fact that practically every major section in the Letter ends on the topic of the return of the Lord (1:10; 2:12; 2:16; 2:19; 3:13; 5:23).

Though Paul does describe the events of the Last Day in response to confusion on this subject, he does not make the Last Day the overarching emphasis of the Letter. He calls the believers to live in the Gospel and to fulfill their calling in the joy of the Holy Spirit. He leaves us an example to follow: know the truths about Christ's return but do not obsess about them.

As you read 1 Thessalonians, reflect on Paul's pastoral concern for these new believers and also his thoughtful and comforting instruction. He shows great concern for their care and establishment in the Gospel, which is also what we need most today.

Outline

I. The Greeting (1:1)

II. Thanksgiving for the Congregation at Thessalonica (1:2–3:13)
   A. The Conversion of the Thessalonians (1:2–10)
   B. Paul's Ministry in Thessalonica (2:1–12)
   C. The Word under Persecution (2:13–16)
   D. Separations and Reestablishing Contact (2:17–3:10)
   E. Prayer (3:11–13)

III. Exhortations (4:1–5:22)
   A. Introduction (4:1–2)
   B. On Marriage (4:3–8)
   C. On Brotherly Love and Self-Sufficiency (4:9–12)
   D. On Clarifying Concerns about the End Times (4:13–5:11)
      1. Those who have fallen asleep (4:13–18)
      2. The coming of the day of the Lord (5:1–11)
   E. On Life in the Congregation (5:12–22)
      1. Pastoral care among the congregation (5:12–15)
      2. The evaluation of prophecy (5:16–22)

IV. Conclusion (5:23–28)

PART 1

GREETING AND THANKSGIVING (CH. 1–3)

The Greeting (1:1)

ESV	KJV
1 ¹Paul, Silvanus, and Timothy, To the church of the Thessalonians in God the Father and the Lord Jesus Christ: Grace to you and peace.	1 ¹Paul, and Silvanus, and Timotheus, unto the church of the Thessalonians which is in God the Father and in the Lord Jesus Christ: Grace be unto you, and peace, from God our Father, and the Lord Jesus Christ.

1:1 In the introduction to Colossians, we noted some basic characteristics of Greek letter writing, which Paul also included here in his Letter to the Thessalonians. (See the introduction to Col 1:1–2 on how Paul begins his Letters.) However, it is also helpful to notice how Paul introduces this Letter to the church of the Thessalonians differently. For example, to the deeply troubled and heresy-threatened congregation at Colossae, Paul began by emphasizing his calling as an apostle. Here he made no mention of that authority, since he would describe further on how fully the Thessalonians received and retained the Word of God from him. This and other points in the Letter show that the situation at Colossae was more troubling than the situation at Thessalonica, though the latter congregation still had its struggles. Bengel wrote,

> "Paul, in this epistle, which was the first of all he wrote, uses neither the title of an apostle, nor any other, because he writes most familiarly to the godly Thessalonians, who did not require a preface regarding his apostolic authority" (Bengel IV:189).

Silvanus, and Timothy. When Paul would write to a congregation, he rarely did so in his own name alone since he saw himself as a leader among brothers in ministry. Both of these men were trusted co-workers who accompanied Paul in the proclamation of the Gospel. Though separated from the apostle for a while, they were now reunited with him in Corinth. They had visited with him in Thessalonica in AD 49 (cf. Ac 17:1–14). Paul selected both of them for his second missionary journey (Ac 15:36–40; 16:1–5). *Silvanus.* Also known as Silas, he was a leading member of the church in Jerusalem and a proclaimer of God's Word. After the Jerusalem Council, he accompanied Paul to Antioch to deliver the Council's decision (Ac 15, especially v. 22). During their travels together, they met Timothy in Lystra. *Timothy.* We already learned about Timothy in the introduction to Colossians (see 1:1), so we recall only the basics here. Timothy was the son of a Greek man and a Jewish woman (cf. Ac 16:1). His mother had become a Christian a few years earlier when Paul and Barnabas preached in the city. He served as a representative for the apostle. *Thessalonians.* In the first century, Thessalonica was the capital city of the Roman province of Macedonia, the territory from which Alexander the Great arose, north of ancient Greece. At that time, Thessalonica was the largest city on the Greek Peninsula. Today it is called Thessaloniki (or Salonika) and is located on the Thermaic Gulf in modern Greece. *in God the Father and the Lord Jesus Christ.* While Paul frequently used the phrase "in Christ" (on which see the note at Col 1:2), this passage is one of the few places in his Letters where he used the expression "in God." The phrase "in God" denotes that when one is "in Christ," one has the same intimate relationship with God the Father (cf. 1Jn 2:23–25). This is because Jesus is equal to the Father according to His divine nature, and because we can come to the Father only through Jesus Christ (as noted in Jn 14:6). *Lord.* See the note at Col 1:3. The first specific mention of the Holy Spirit in the Letter soon occurs, in 1:5. Wherever God the Father and the Lord Jesus Christ are found, the Holy Spirit is also there. At the end of the verse, most later Greek manuscripts include an additional phrase (cf. KJV) that likely came into the mind of the scribes as they were used to writing it from Paul's other introductions to Letters (e.g. Eph 1:2; Php 1:2).

1:1 in Devotion and Prayer As a good shepherd, Paul wanted to keep in touch with the flock of God and guide them in the way of grace and peace. Labor in God's kingdom is not a one-man job. Paul drew with him colleagues who could help. He reached out to persons in the local congregation. As we consider our calling in our congregations today, we must not forget to visit and follow up with those who are in Christ Jesus. We work together in God's kingdom by joining hands with other brothers and sisters and trusting that God is at work in and through them. God the Father and the Lord Jesus Christ will sustain the Church and carry it in the palm of His hand. • Lord, thank You that the Church is rooted in You and not in feeble human beings. Yet as feeble human beings, as brothers and sisters in Christ, we are blessed by You through each others' service. Help us to join hands, as did Paul, Silas, and Timothy, and labor together in Your kingdom. Amen.

The Conversion of the Thessalonians (1:2–10)

ESV	KJV
[2]We give thanks to God always for all of you, constantly mentioning you in our prayers, [3]remembering before our God and Father your work of faith and labor of love and steadfastness of hope in our Lord Jesus Christ. [4]For we know, brothers loved by God, that he has chosen you, [5]because our gospel came to you not only in word, but also in power and in the Holy Spirit and with full conviction. You know what kind of men we proved to be among you for your sake. [6]And you became imitators of us and of the Lord, for you received the word in much affliction, with the joy of the Holy Spirit, [7]so that you became an example to all the believers in Macedonia and in Achaia. [8]For not only has the word of the Lord sounded forth from you in Macedonia and Achaia, but your faith in God has gone forth everywhere, so that we need not say anything.	[2]We give thanks to God always for you all, making mention of you in our prayers; [3]Remembering without ceasing your work of faith, and labour of love, and patience of hope in our Lord Jesus Christ, in the sight of God and our Father; [4]Knowing, brethren beloved, your election of God. [5]For our gospel came not unto you in word only, but also in power, and in the Holy Ghost, and in much assurance; as ye know what manner of men we were among you for your sake. [6]And ye became followers of us, and of the Lord, having received the word in much affliction, with joy of the Holy Ghost. [7]So that ye were ensamples to all that believe in Macedonia and Achaia. [8]For from you sounded out the word of the Lord not only in Macedonia and Achaia, but also in every place your faith to God-ward is spread abroad; so that we need not to speak any thing.

⁹For they themselves report concerning us the kind of reception we had among you, and how you turned to God from idols to serve the living and true God, ¹⁰and to wait for his Son from heaven, whom he raised from the dead, Jesus who delivers us from the wrath to come.

⁹For they themselves shew of us what manner of entering in we had unto you, and how ye turned to God from idols to serve the living and true God;
¹⁰And to wait for his Son from heaven, whom he raised from the dead, even Jesus, which delivered us from the wrath to come.

Introduction to 1:2–10 Faith, as something invisible to our eyes, is a bit mysterious. Often people have wondered how to have faith and what it means to have faith. Yet seeing faith at work in a person's life is remarkable and one of the most inspiring things a fellow Christian can witness. As Paul described here how the Thessalonians came to faith, he delved into the profound mystery of the Holy Spirit's work as a person of the Holy Trinity. As you read these opening verses, consider your own experience and the persons God used to bring you to faith. Think about how you might emulate their good example and put that into practice in your life today. Remember that just as the Holy Spirit worked through the powerful Gospel of Jesus Christ to bring Paul's first readers to faith, so He works likewise in the lives of all those who come to believe in the Lord Jesus Christ.

1:2 *thanks.* See the introduction to 2Th 1:3–4. Just as a tree is known by its leaves, flowers, and ultimately its fruit, so Christian faith is recognized by the flourishing life and fruit it bears among believers. Luther wrote,

> Christ says, "A bad tree does not make good fruits; a good tree does not make bad fruits" [Matt. 7:18]. Now it is clear that the fruits do not bear the tree, nor does the tree grow on the fruits. On the contrary, the trees bear the fruits, and the fruits grow on the trees. As it is necessary that trees exist prior to their fruits, and as the fruits do not make the trees either good or bad—on the contrary, the same sorts of trees make the same sorts of fruits—so it is necessary that the person itself of the man be good or bad first before he does a good or bad work. His works do not make him bad or good, but he himself makes his works either bad or good. (*Christian Freedom* [St. Louis: Concordia, 2012] 67)

The apostle here gives thanks for the fruit of faith God produced in the lives of the Thessalonians (see v. 3), which inspired him to pray. Faith is contagious this way, spreading from person to person as they share the Word. *constantly mentioning.* Paul and his co-workers were in a constant attitude of prayer, even when they were not consciously vocalizing or thinking prayers to God. How does this work? Of course, the apostle would not have us with hands folded and eyes closed while we drive or operate heavy equipment! Yet faith should stir us to talk to God, to flow our thoughts and even verbally express our words toward Him in every circumstance and at every opportunity. When it comes to prayer, Paul is something of a name dropper. He can't help saying, "Lord, did you notice the Thessalonians? . . . Did you see what happened among them?" And rehearse what he has seen and heard with thanks.

1:3 *faith . . . love . . . hope.* The big three. These are all enduring gifts of the Holy Spirit and characteristics of the Christian life. Faith shows itself in works, the greatest of which is love (1Co 13) that labors for others. Faith also gives us hope for the future, and such hope gives us steadfastness in the face of adversity. When you are thinking about bearing witness to someone about the Gospel but unsure about what to say to them, perhaps consider the matter in view of faith, love, and hope. Ask yourself, "How would I encourage this person toward faith? How would I show this person God's love today? What would I hope for this person's life now practically and eternally?" These thoughts should guide you toward more fruitful witness.

1:4 *brothers.* This was a common NT name for fellow members of God's family, the Church (Rm 8:29; Eph 6:23). See note, Col 1:2. As conflicts and disagreements arise in your congregation, remember this word and relationship. Think of your fellow members as "brothers loved by God" when you are trying to love them in challenging times. When the heat of challenge is on, gently address them as "brothers" or "sisters" so that they too may remember the family bond created by faith in the Gospel. *chosen.* Their faith and love are evidence that God chose the Thessalonians for salvation through the Gospel (v. 5); see further the notes at 2Th 2:13–14. Paul was referring to one of the great themes in his Letters, the mystery of election or predestination in Christ. Paul did not speak of election in the abstract but noted its concrete effects in Christians' daily lives due to the Gospel's impact. Note that he ultimately regarded it as a mystery of God that we cannot figure out with our limited reason (cf. Rm 11:33–36, which concludes an extended presentation on election). Bengel wrote,

> There is a kind of unmingled sweetness in this epistle, which, by a reader not accustomed to the expression of sweet affections, is less relished than the others, that act upon the palate with a certain degree of harshness. The expectation of the coming of Christ among the Thessalonians was unclouded. So exalted was their condition, and so clear of impediments and encumbrances was the state of Christianity among them, that they were able hourly to look for the Lord Jesus. (Bengel IV:190)

1:5 *our gospel.* Paul received the Gospel from the Lord, but it is the same message preached by the other apostles (1Co 15:3; Gal 2:9). Modern interpreters sometimes wish to pit the message of Peter against that of Paul as though there was more than one Gospel among the apostles. But these ideas come from theories about society and cultural movements and not from the facts. In Ac 15 we see the apostles working through questions of doctrine and practice together and expressing a common faith. Paul could write, with his colleagues, about "our" Gospel because of his personal investment in it as a preacher and teacher. *power.* The good news of our Lord Jesus Christ is more than mere words; it always has power to change lives (Heb 4:12). The Word's power may be demonstrated in visible, supernatural miracles, particularly in regions where the Gospel is being preached for the first time. But even if such miracles are not observed, the powerful Gospel of Christ is always the cause of the miracle of someone coming to saving faith in Jesus. This is in fact the greatest power of the Gospel—its ability to deliver someone from evil and thereby to transform their whole life. *Holy Spirit.* Jesus said the Spirit would testify about Him. The Spirit is always present when the Gospel is preached (cf. Jn 15:26), and He is the source of the Gospel's power. Note the references to all three persons of the Holy Trinity in vv. 3–4. *full conviction.* In the NT (see Col 2:2; Heb 6:11; 10:22) this expression indicates that through faith in Christ the Thessalonians had full conviction of the truth of the Gospel. There was not a long delay or period of assimilating the Gospel message as happens in some cases. We see in the Gospels that at times Jesus rebuked the disciples for their "little faith" since they were slow to trust His promises and teaching. Whether quickly or slowly, the Holy Spirit grants confidence/trust for eternity life through the Gospel.

The Holy Spirit persuades and convicts on the basis of Christ's accomplished work. Certainly "full conviction" is not some higher level of faith that we produce in ourselves. Only by the Spirit's power do we overcome doubt and unbelief and trust in Christ with saving faith.

1:6 *imitators.* In modern society there is great emphasis on uniqueness. People are supposed to find their own way, painters are to develop a fresh approach, singers and musicians must produce a unique sound (whether good or bad) in order to be heard and recognized. And heaven help us, theologians are only remembered and studied if they introduce something unheard of. But when it comes to making disciples, Paul does not share this modern concern with uniqueness. In v. 3 Paul commented on the Thessalonians' work but here he tells us more specifically about it. The Thessalonians followed Christ's and the apostles' examples by gladly suffering persecution for the sake of their faith in the Gospel (1Co 11:1). What is unique about them is their glad reception of the Word and tenacious hold upon it under trying circumstances that would cause other people to give up and let go. Here is an example for us to imitate. (See also the note at 2:14.) *much affliction.* The degree is important to the Thessalonian experience. They had "much" trouble or hardship, which Christians may face due to their faith and witness (see further the note at Col 1:24). We know from the Book of Acts that some persons in the Jewish community stirred up a mob against Paul's hosts in Thessalonica (Ac 17:1–9). It is not clear whether Paul had further trouble in mind, though his emphasis on the point may suggest just that.

1:7 Paul referred to the fact that Rome had divided the Greek Peninsula into two provinces, Macedonia (north) and Achaia (south). *example.* In the previous verse, Paul referred to the example that he had set for these new believers. Then he drew them alongside himself as fellow Christians and servants of the Word. By their patience and even joy in suffering, the Thessalonians have provided for others an example that they may imitate. The Christian characteristics of faith, love, and hope were stamped upon them in palpable form.

1:8 *sounded forth.* The Greek term appears only here in the NT but is used in other literature to describe thunder or the rapid spread of a rumor. The good news echoes from Macedonia. Paul did not flatter them (cf. 2:5–6). As in the popular saying "Actions speak louder than words," news of the Thessalonians' faith, love, and hope rooted in the Gospel spread far wider than their immediate environment. The Thessalonians functioned as a missionary church through proclamation and through their lives that resounded with the Gospel they received. As a consequence (and with irony), Paul and his colleagues could be silent. Like proud parents or teachers, they could for a moment sit back and listen with joyful humility to the confession of faith they had first recited to the Thessalonians.

1:9 *they.* Believers throughout the church report on the faithfulness of the Thessalonians. As the capital city of the province, Thessalonica likely had a steady stream of visitors from the surrounding area, which made it possible for the congregation to share God's Word with those who had not yet believed as well as sharing their good example with those who had believed. *from idols.* We know from Ac 17 that both Jews and Gentiles were among those at Thessalonica who believed the Gospel. Before the Gospel came to them, the Gentile Thessalonians worshiped idols. Forsaking idol worship and coming to the true and living God was important evidence of true conversion in the first century—they were radically departing from the custom of the day. Since Paul broadly associated idol worship with the former lives of those in the congregation, this may mean that the congregation now had many more Gentiles than Jews. *serve.* God is served first of all when we worship Him (e.g., "worship service") and again when we proclaim His Word. Finally, He is served when we have mercy upon others through acts of kindness and love. *living . . . God.* This title from the OT became more popular during Israel's time in exile and under the rule of the Ptolemies and the Seleucids in the intertestamental period. The more that the Jews were exposed to pagan idolatry beyond Canaan, the more they emphasized that their God, the true God, was alive and not lifeless wood and stone. Calvin wrote,

> In the detail which follows, he shews, first, what the condition of mankind is before the Lord enlightens them by the doctrine of his gospel; and farther, for what end he would have us instructed, and what is the fruit of the gospel. For although all do not worship idols, all are nevertheless addicted to idolatry, and are immersed in blindness and madness. Hence, it is owing to the kindness of God, that we are exempted from the impostures of the devil, and every kind of superstition. Some, indeed, he converts earlier, others later, but as alienation is common to all, it is necessary that we be converted to God, before we can serve God. From this, also we gather the essence and nature of true faith, inasmuch as no one gives due credit to God but the man, who renouncing the

vanity of his own understanding, embraces and receives the pure worship of God. (Calvin 245)

1:10 *to wait for His Son.* The early Christians actively expected the second coming of our Lord. The NT teaches that since the completion of the work of Christ we have been in the Last Days (e.g., Ac 2:16–17; 2Tm 3:1–5), so that the return of Christ could take place at any moment. Hence, all Christians should live as though their Lord could return at any time, for indeed He can. Although they were waiting for Him, they were not to be idle but serving (v. 9) diligently in faith, love, and hope. *raised . . . delivers.* The resurrection of Christ was the completion of His redemptive work and confirmation that His death on the cross had been sufficient to obtain the world's forgiveness and salvation. This salvation will be brought to its consummation at the Last Day, when Jesus will raise His people from their graves and gather them with believers still living to the splendor of eternal life (see 4:13–18). *wrath.* This refers to the resurrection to eternal judgment that will come upon the unbelieving when Christ comes again. To those who doubt the existence of hell (2Th 1:8) as a prison to separate the wicked from the righteous, Paul added a reminder that Jesus is coming again in both judgment and salvation. See also the note at 2:16.

1:2–10 in Devotion and Prayer The Thessalonians became model Christians in words and deeds due to the impact of the Gospel in their lives and the fruit of the Spirit demonstrated in faith, love, and hope. Paul praised God not only for their good deeds but especially for the resounding Word of the Lord that they had sounded throughout the region. They actively shared the Gospel of Jesus Christ, setting a marvelous example for all. Compared to the Thessalonians, we appear much poorer in our faith, labor of love, and steadfastness of hope. Even without hardship or persecution, we are too slow to confess our faith and live it out in love. Yet the Lord knows each one of us and our specific situation. He knows our strengths, our weaknesses, and also our too deeply hidden desire to serve Him boldly. His Spirit has created our faith and He is fully able to give us power and full conviction. Despite our weaknesses and failings, His unfailing love and forgiveness will sustain us to be His witnesses. • Thank You, Lord, for the bold and faith-filled life You gave to the Thessalonians. Lead us to imitate their great faith. Make us also exemplary witnesses for the Gospel, so that Your name may be glorified far beyond our community. Amen.

Paul's Ministry in Thessalonica (2:1–12)

ESV	KJV
2 ¹For you yourselves know, brothers, that our coming to you was not in vain. ²But though we had already suffered and been shamefully treated at Philippi, as you know, we had boldness in our God to declare to you the gospel of God in the midst of much conflict. ³For our appeal does not spring from error or impurity or any attempt to deceive, ⁴but just as we have been approved by God to be entrusted with the gospel, so we speak, not to please man, but to please God who tests our hearts. ⁵For we never came with words of flattery, as you know, nor with a pretext for greed— God is witness. ⁶Nor did we seek glory from people, whether from you or from others, though we could have made demands as apostles of Christ. ⁷But we were gentle among you, like a nursing mother taking care of her own children. ⁸So, being affectionately desirous of you, we were ready to share with you not only the gospel of God but also our own selves, because you had become very dear to us. ⁹For you remember, brothers, our labor and toil: we worked night and day, that we might not be a burden to any of you, while we proclaimed to you the gospel of God. ¹⁰You are witnesses, and God also, how holy and righteous and blameless was our conduct toward you believers. ¹¹For you know how, like a father with his children, ¹²we exhorted each one of you and encouraged you and charged you to walk in a manner worthy of God, who calls you into his own kingdom and glory.	2 ¹For yourselves, brethren, know our entrance in unto you, that it was not in vain: ²But even after that we had suffered before, and were shamefully entreated, as ye know, at Philippi, we were bold in our God to speak unto you the gospel of God with much contention. ³For our exhortation was not of deceit, nor of uncleanness, nor in guile: ⁴But as we were allowed of God to be put in trust with the gospel, even so we speak; not as pleasing men, but God, which trieth our hearts. ⁵For neither at any time used we flattering words, as ye know, nor a cloke of covetousness; God is witness: ⁶Nor of men sought we glory, neither of you, nor yet of others, when we might have been burdensome, as the apostles of Christ. ⁷But we were gentle among you, even as a nurse cherisheth her children: ⁸So being affectionately desirous of you, we were willing to have imparted unto you, not the gospel of God only, but also our own souls, because ye were dear unto us. ⁹For ye remember, brethren, our labour and travail: for labouring night and day, because we would not be chargeable unto any of you, we preached unto you the gospel of God. ¹⁰Ye are witnesses, and God also, how holily and justly and unblameably we behaved ourselves among you that believe: ¹¹As ye know how we exhorted and comforted and charged every one of you, as a father doth his children, ¹²That ye would walk worthy of God, who hath called you unto his kingdom and glory.

Introduction to 2:1–16 To this point in the Letter, Paul has emphasized the blessed and broad public results of the Gospel in the lives of the Thessalonians. He has praised them highly for their grasp of the Gospel and their willingness to share it far beyond their congregation and their borders. But now Paul would bring his message home. He wrote privately, intimately with imagery from the tenderest moments of family life. In this section Paul's experience, inner being, motives, and love toward the Thessalonian Christians are laid bare. He reminded the Thessalonians of the trying circumstances when he brought them the Gospel with character and integrity (vv. 1–8). He wrote about how he conducted himself (vv. 9–12). He commended the Thessalonians for receiving the Gospel preached by him as the Word of God and for enduring persecution for its sake (vv. 13–16). Portions of Paul's words may sound boastful. But realize that they also portray the hard work, self-sacrifice, and integrity with which Paul and his colleagues conducted themselves in service to the congregation since these were necessary elements of their teaching— lives that illustrated the Gospel.

2:1 *brothers.* Paul often addressed the readers of his Letters with this family term, which illustrates the intimacy of churchly life for the earliest Christians. Paul's Letters were publicly read in the congregations that received them (Col 4:6; 1Th 5:27). So the address to brothers does not necessarily exclude women, who would be present to hear the public readings. However, translations that automatically extend Paul's word "brothers" to include women and render it "brothers and sisters," are adding things to the text that may be misleading. *coming.* Paul visited Thessalonica during his second missionary journey (AD 49–51). This Letter was written near the end of that journey so he was not long separated from the congregation when he composed this. *not in vain.* Through Paul's proclamation of the Gospel, a number of Jews and Greeks came to the Christian faith (Ac 17:1–4) and shortly established a vibrant congregation.

2:2 *suffered.* Paul and Silas were unjustly beaten and imprisoned in Philippi (Ac 16:19–24). Other conflicts arose in nearly every city where they proclaimed the surprising message that Jesus is the Christ. *conflict.* The missionaries narrowly escaped the search made for them in Thessalonica. Instead, their host and some of the Christian brothers were mistreated (Ac 17:5–10). The difficulties that Paul and Silas experienced were a testimony to their commitment and sincerity (2:5–6), which set them in contrast to many other religious teachers in the ancient world (2:3). When the crowd at Thessalonica complained about their preaching, they said, "These men . . . have turned the world upside down" (Ac 17:6). The Gospel, firmly grasped and believed, fills one with boldness. In cases where Christians find themselves or their congregations anemic in bearing witness and doing good works, the cure is simply to return to the Gospel. It is the source of God-given boldness in believers.

2:3 The Greeks had a long tradition of traveling or "peripatetic" teachers who might show up unexpectedly in a community to seek students for their philosophy. Some were reputable but others were not. As a result, persons in this region were accustomed to hearing the latest ideas from strangers. Just as a faithful pastor today may need to establish his credibility with his hearers due to their jaded experience with false shepherds or the antics of radio and TV preachers, so Paul needed to remind people that he and his colleagues were different. There were many false teachers of religion and philosophy in the Greco-Roman world of the time who deceived people and made great claims for personal gains. In this passage, Paul distanced himself from such deceivers.

2:4 *approved.* This word refers to the result after a test. God tested Paul and then entrusted the preaching of the Gospel to him. Although every believer is called to share God's Word (Ps 145), not every believer is entrusted with the public proclamation of that Word as happened with the apostles in the first century and as happens today with pastors and teachers. Paul could point to his experience with Jesus (Ac 9) as well as his reception among the other apostles and leaders of the Early Church (Ac 15; Gal 2:1–10) as the basis for his public ministry. *tests our hearts.* Paul preached in constant awareness of his accountability before God for his words. Notice that Paul wrote about "hearts" rather than minds or brains. This is not because knowledge is unimportant—it is. But the faithful public minister thrives by trust in God and not by having God or the congregation figured out. The mysteries of the Word of God sufficiently test our minds; the trials of serving test our hearts.

2:5 Paul's opponents conducted themselves for flattery and praise. Paul, however, as the Lord's true servant, wanted to please God, who searches the heart (2:4; Rm 8:27), unlike people, who see only what is outside. Calvin wrote,

He makes mention here of two vices, from which he declares himself to be exempt, and, in doing so, teaches that the servants of Christ should stand aloof from them. Thus, if we would distinguish the genuine servants of Christ from those that are pretended and spurious, they must be tried according to this rule, and every one that would serve Christ aright must also conform his aims and actions to the same rule. For where avarice and ambition reign, innumerable corruptions follow, and the whole man passes away into vanity, for these are the two sources from which the corruption of the whole ministry takes place. (Calvin 251)

2:6 Paul reminded them that it was within his dignity, as one called by the Lord of heaven and earth, to demand their support, favor, and adulation. Leaders of this era might parade through the streets to gain attention and stir up their followers to frenzied obedience. Visiting dignitaries would conduct themselves with pompous displays in order to emphasize their importance and to make the persons they visited also feel important. Paul left all such glory aside and went right to the heart of the matter—the Gospel of Jesus, who alone is worthy of our faith and praise. On the "glory" of apostleship, see note, Col 1:1. Although Paul and his fellow workers could request pay, thanks, and greater public recognition (see 2:9 and note), they did not seek these but focused on the service to which God called them (cf. 2Co 11:7).

2:7 *gentle.* Greek *epioi.* Some ancient manuscripts have "infants" (Greek *nepioi*; a one letter difference!). This is one of those rare cases where it is very difficult to decide between possible readings. The earliest Greek manuscripts were written very tightly in order to save precious space on expensive paper. The scribes would run one word right after the other asIamillustratinghere. In the Greek text of v. 7, the word just before "gentle" has an "n" at the end. It would be easy for a scribe copying the manuscript to look at the tightly packed words and write an extra "n" that changed "gentle" to "infants." In either case, the term describes the intimate care Paul rendered to the Thessalonians. *nursing mother.* Paul's imagery in this verse sharply contrasts with the honors he was describing earlier. In vv. 5–6 he mentions glory and the demands and privileges that go with public office. Here he steps out of the public eye and into the privacy of the home where mother and child, in the most gentle intimacy, sustain the family bond. It is just such a bond that Paul nurtured in this intimate portion of his letter, which also gives us a picture of the gentleness of spiritual care when one believer visits another out of the public eye in an effort to share the peace of Christ and the Word of life, which sustains the soul (cf. how Paul described the Word in 1Co 3:2). The Thessalonians, as recent believers, were growing wonderfully, yet would retain some frailness of faith and dependency on their leaders.

2:8 *affectionately desirous.* The Greek word is very rare but may come from the nursing relationship Paul referenced in v. 7. *also our own selves.* Cf. Jn 15:13. The KJV renders more literally with the word "soul." Paul was willing to risk his life to preach the Gospel in hostile environments. Acts describes him doing so on numerous occasions and, indeed, from the beginning of his ministry. A popular maxim in public speaking is that the speaker is the message. Everything you are and do reinforces the message that you advance. Paul noted that as the Gospel went forth from his heart and mind, he went with it in a self-sacrificing love.

2:9 *worked.* Paul and his colleagues did not depend upon the support of others, even though they were entitled to it (1Co 9:14; Gal 6:6). Instead, we read in other places that Paul plied his trade as a tentmaker (Ac 18:3; see also 2Co 11:9; 2Th 3:8). However, he would accept voluntary offerings given in support of his work (Php 4:14–18). *night and day.* Apparently Paul and his colleagues worked their trade during the business hours of the day and shared the Word with people into the evening (cf. an example in Ac 20:7–16). They did not receive pay from the congregation so as to remove all potential obstacles to their message and to provide the Thessalonians with every advantage in establishing a congregation. In this we see the depth of their dedication. For Paul, ministry was certainly more than a job he pursued.

2:10 Paul was not boasting or claiming perfection. Instead, his words are to be understood as a defense of the integrity of their ministry among the Thessalonians (cf. 2:2, 5–6). It is noteworthy that Paul appealed not only to witnesses among the Thessalonians, who apparently would come forward quickly in support of him, but he also appealed to God as his witness. He and his colleagues lived and served ever conscious that the omnipresent God was with them at each step and could defend their reputation if that became necessary. As in v. 6, Paul wrote here in a public manner, since witnesses were used in legal proceedings.

2:11 *father with his children.* Again Paul turned away from the crowded streets and marketplace to illustrate his point from the family setting. See the maternal example in v. 7. Paul added a paternal example to describe his warnings and instructions. He was their "father" in Christ through his ministry of the Word (1Co 4:15).

2:12 *exhorted . . . encouraged.* As a father prepares his children to leave the home, maintain their integrity, and represent the household, so Paul spoke to the Thessalonians who would go forth to share Christ with others around the city and around the region. As the blessed Trinity (1:2–7) equipped and sent him out into the world with the Gospel, Paul equipped the Thessalonians with his words. *walk.* The Greek term is *peripateo;* it is used here in the ethical sense to mean "conduct yourself." See further the note at Col 1:10. The Thessalonians are admonished to demonstrate a character compatible with God's will, i.e., the revealed Word of God. Christians, like children who never outgrow the counsel of their father nor the nurturing love of their mother, continue to benefit from the counsel of God recorded in His Word. By faith they bear His likeness before the world. *kingdom.* As in the four Gospels this word here does not designate a place but rather God's activity in Christ of restoring us to a right relationship with Him (see further the note at Col 1:14). This restored relationship will come in its fullness when all people of God will be resurrected and Christ will hand over the kingdom to God (1Co 15:23–28). God's kingdom, however, is not limited to the future (Rm 14:17). So as God's people step out of their homes and into the streets of this world, they do not leave the ways of the kingdom of God behind. When they step out the doors of their churches, they remain citizens of an eternal reign and kingdom to which even our most grand church buildings weakly testify. *glory.* See the note at Col 1:27; see also Rm 8:18. Paul pointed his readers to the final resurrection, when we will share in the glory of God's presence forever.

The Word under Persecution (2:13–16)

ESV	KJV
¹³And we also thank God constantly for this, that when you received the word of God, which you heard from us, you accepted it not as the word of men but as what it really is, the word of God, which is at work in you believers. ¹⁴For you, brothers, became imitators of the churches of God in Christ Jesus that are in Judea. For you suffered the same things from your own countrymen as they did from the Jews, ¹⁵who killed both the Lord Jesus and the prophets, and drove us out, and displease God and oppose all mankind ¹⁶by hindering us from speaking to the Gentiles that they might be saved—so as always to fill up the measure of their sins. But God's wrath has come upon them at last!	¹³For this cause also thank we God without ceasing, because, when ye received the word of God which ye heard of us, ye received it not as the word of men, but as it is in truth, the word of God, which effectually worketh also in you that believe. ¹⁴For ye, brethren, became followers of the churches of God which in Judaea are in Christ Jesus: for ye also have suffered like things of your own countrymen, even as they have of the Jews: ¹⁵Who both killed the Lord Jesus, and their own prophets, and have persecuted us; and they please not God, and are contrary to all men: ¹⁶Forbidding us to speak to the Gentiles that they might be saved, to fill up their sins alway: for the wrath is come upon them to the uttermost.

2:13 *word of God*. The message Paul preached was not his own creation. He received it from the Lord to pass on to faithful persons who were able to preserve and teach it (1Co 15:3; Gal 1:11; 2Tm 2:2). See further the note at 2Th 2:15. We should not pass too quickly over this important point. Our ears are filled with words these days. From the moment we awake in the morning, we may click on the radio or TV. An abundance of type adorns our shelves and stuffs our mail boxes and email inboxes. A world of words is available to us at the click of a button on devices not only found in our offices but now on our own persons. In such a word-rich environment, we may easily hear the Law and the Gospel as just more messages to file, delete, process, or ignore. We may regard these words as not much different from mere human words, which are powerless to accomplish what they say. The Thessalonians in Paul's day did not experience the same word clutter that we have today, yet they could rightly wonder how the things Paul had to say would prove any different from the words of the next travelling teacher or the tent mender in the next stall at the marketplace. Praise be to God, they received the Word from Paul and his colleagues as something absolutely unique among all the other words and voices that they had ever heard. Gerhard wrote,

> The Word of God is compared to "a seed" (Luke 8:1; 1 Pet. 1:23), but a seed has in itself an internal power to bear fruit (Mark 4:28). It is compared to "a fire" (Jer. 23:29), but fire has an internal power to burn. So also the Word of God, preached or written, has a power of the same kind to change and kindle hearts spiritually. Consequently, the disciples confess that "their hearts burned" when Christ was interpreting Scripture to them (Luke 24:32). Note in this passage that the written Word of God declared and explained by Christ gave forth that power. The apostle's word was taken without any witness or mandate of the Church "as the Word of God Himself" (1 Thess. 2:13). (Gerhard E 1.42)

In the same way, Lord, grant that we hear, read, and receive Your Word apart from every other message in our too busy lives. *which is at work*. The Greek term is *energetai*, which could also be translated "working effectively." It is the source of our English word "energy." The Lord's Word will produce visible fruit among those who listen and believe (Is 55:10–11). Such a life-changing effect cannot be produced by mere human words. The Greek could also be translated "WHO is at work" (referring to God); perhaps Paul was inspired to write in this way, thereby making the point that God works through His Word. See further the notes at 1:3–5. Notice also the little word "is." It speaks in the present tense—the Word of God is at work right now, Paul wrote to the Thessalonians. Realize that the same is true for us right now. As you read the Letter from the apostle and as you take in its message of sin and grace, promise and hope, that word is at work in your life as a believer. By faith the Word that you receive—unfiltered from the Father who exhorts and encourages (v. 12), filtered from the word clutter that clamors and nags—is working your deliverance from every evil of body and soul. It aims to deliver you from the kingdom of this world to that kingdom which has no end.

2:14 *imitators*. The Greek word is *mimetai*, the source of the English word "mimic" (see note, 1:6). Like the churches of Judea that suffered persecution, the Thessalonians had passed through an experience of persecution. The troubles described in Ac 17:1–9 may not give us a complete picture of the types of hardship they suffered since Paul is comparing them to a place and circumstance that included very intense persecution. Bengel wrote,

> The sameness of the fruit, the sameness of the afflictions, the sameness of the experimental proofs and characteristics of believers, in all places and at all times, afford an excellent criterion of the truth of the Gospel. (Bengel 196)

Judea. Here the term refers to the original churches in Jerusalem. Following the ridicule of the crowds and intimidation from public officials (Ac 2, 4), the believers in Judea were dispersed after the martyrdom of Stephen and subsequent persecution (Ac 8:1). There is no mention of martyrdom in the persecution at Thessalonica. However, the sufferings they received from their countrymen (Ac 17:1–9), if they did not involve the giving up of life, might still compare with those things the earliest Christians endured at the hands of their fellow Jews. On suffering and persecution in the Christian life, see the note at Col 1:24. *Jews.* The context, in particular 2:15, makes it plain that Paul was referring to certain Jews in particular; the apostle was not making a blanket condemnation of all Jews, as he gladly acknowledged that he himself was a Jew (Rm 9–11; Php 3:4–6; cf. Col 4:11). In the past, some angry Christians have sinfully described Jews as "Christ killers" in an effort to stir up other Christians in public opposition to Jews in their community or nation. Such shrill rhetoric and hate-filled distortion of history has no place in the Christian Church. No passage of Scripture, including this one, maintains that the Jewish people as a whole are more culpable in the death of our Lord than anyone else (e.g., see Rm 9:1–5; 1Co 2:8). The sin of condemning Christ to crucifixion belongs, on the one hand, to those Jews and Romans who cooperated in Jesus' execution. On the other hand, it belongs to every sinner whose errant life demands atonement.

2:15 *drove us out.* This is likely a reference to the circumstances at Thessalonica, which caused the brothers there to send Paul and Silas away secretly (Ac 17:10). On an earlier trip to Lystra, Paul was stoned to death by a crowd that the Jews stirred up there. Although God raised up Paul, he must have had little interest in repeating the experience! (Ac 14:19–20). *prophets.* God's ancient people, the Israelites/Jews, had a long history of rejecting, mistreating, and even killing prophets and others God sent to them (Mt 23:34–35; Lk 13:34; Ac 7:52; see also Heb 11:37, which may refer to the prophet Isaiah). That this took place among God's chosen people under the Old Testament should be a sober warning for all Christians: we should not be so arrogant so as to assume that we could never fall into opposing the proclamation and spread of God's Word. In fact, examples from church history and from the Reformation era in particular bear witness to the brutal persecution of one group of professing Christians against another. One thinks, for example, of Henry of Zutphen, an Augustinian monk who lived and studied with Luther at Wittenberg. After Henry left Wittenberg to preach the Gospel in his homeland of the Netherlands, he experienced persecution that ended with a mob burning him at the stake (1524).

2:16 *measure of their sins.* Even beyond rejecting God's Word through unbelief, the opponents at Thessalonica, by hindering the proclamation of the Gospel, had so grievously offended God that they had exhausted his long-suffering patience. They would bring the full measure of His wrath upon themselves. Paul referred to the Old Testament imagery of the "cup of wrath" in which one was forced to drink a brimming cup of punishment that brought on a self-destructive, drunken stupor. Over time, one's sins filled the cup until God, having lost patience, forced one to drink in the consequences of wickedness. See Is 51:17. *wrath has come upon them.* Some scholars have tried to connect this "wrath" with certain historical events that would happen in about 20 years such as the destruction of Jerusalem in AD 70, since v. 15 points especially to the unbelieving residents of Judea. These scholars argue that the verb's past tense would stress the certainty of wrath in the future (in other words, the wrath is so certain, it can be considered as complete). However, while this interpretation might be possible, Paul seems to refer to something present or recent. For example, in AD 49 the emperor Claudius expelled Jews from Rome for squabbling over a "Chrestus," which probably refers to Christ. The Roman Jews' resistance to the Gospel led to their expulsion along with the Jewish Christians they were persecuting (Ac 18). We should remember that besides the sure and future judgment that was to come upon the unbelieving people of Judea, everyone who is not in Christ and opposes His Gospel of grace is under God's wrath (Jn 3:18).

2:1–16 in Devotion and Prayer The apostle's ministry among the Thessalonians is a model of ministry in Christ's name. Paul described his service among them both in terms of public life and the private life of parents who nurture and equip their children to face the world confidently. The Lord wants us to share His Gospel boldly, even if there is suffering or conflict in our path. We should please God and be faithful to His message rather than speak what is pleasing for people to hear. The Lord who commanded His disciples to preach the Gospel to all nations will be with us according to His promise and will enable us to pass through any hardship we may face. The Gospel's truth and power will not change despite our feebleness (2Co 4:7). • Help us, Lord, to confess the Gospel of Christ faithfully. May our life also shine before the world so that the preaching of the Gospel may not be eclipsed by the darkness in our life. Amen.

Separation and Reestablishing Contact (2:17–3:10)

ESV	KJV
[17]But since we were torn away from you, brothers, for a short time, in person not in heart, we endeavored the more eagerly and with great desire to see you face to face, [18]because we wanted to come to you—I, Paul, again and again—but Satan hindered us. [19]For what is our hope or joy or crown of boasting before our Lord Jesus at his coming? Is it not you? [20]For you are our glory and joy. 3 [1]Therefore when we could bear it no longer, we were willing to be left behind at Athens alone, [2]and we sent Timothy, our brother and God's coworker in the gospel of Christ, to establish and exhort you in your faith, [3]that no one be moved by these afflictions. For you yourselves know that we are destined for this. [4]For when we were with you, we kept telling you beforehand that we were to suffer affliction, just as it has come to pass, and just as you know.	[17]But we, brethren, being taken from you for a short time in presence, not in heart, endeavoured the more abundantly to see your face with great desire. [18]Wherefore we would have come unto you, even I Paul, once and again; but Satan hindered us. [19]For what is our hope, or joy, or crown of rejoicing? Are not even ye in the presence of our Lord Jesus Christ at his coming? [20]For ye are our glory and joy. 3 [1]Wherefore when we could no longer forbear, we thought it good to be left at Athens alone; [2]And sent Timotheus, our brother, and minister of God, and our fellow labourer in the gospel of Christ, to establish you, and to comfort you concerning your faith: [3]That no man should be moved by these afflictions: for yourselves know that we are appointed thereunto. [4]For verily, when we were with you, we told you before that we should suffer tribulation; even as it came to pass, and ye know.

⁵For this reason, when I could bear it no longer, I sent to learn about your faith, for fear that somehow the tempter had tempted you and our labor would be in vain.

⁶But now that Timothy has come to us from you, and has brought us the good news of your faith and love and reported that you always remember us kindly and long to see us, as we long to see you—⁷for this reason, brothers, in all our distress and affliction we have been comforted about you through your faith. ⁸For now we live, if you are standing fast in the Lord. ⁹For what thanksgiving can we return to God for you, for all the joy that we feel for your sake before our God, ¹⁰as we pray most earnestly night and day that we may see you face to face and supply what is lacking in your faith?

⁵For this cause, when I could no longer forbear, I sent to know your faith, lest by some means the tempter have tempted you, and our labour be in vain.

⁶But now when Timotheus came from you unto us, and brought us good tidings of your faith and charity, and that ye have good remembrance of us always, desiring greatly to see us, as we also to see you:

⁷Therefore, brethren, we were comforted over you in all our affliction and distress by your faith:

⁸For now we live, if ye stand fast in the Lord.

⁹For what thanks can we render to God again for you, for all the joy wherewith we joy for your sakes before our God;

¹⁰Night and day praying exceedingly that we might see your face, and might perfect that which is lacking in your faith?

Introduction to 2:17–3:10 Paul next recounted what recently took place since he left Thessalonica. The passion with which Paul wrote illustrates the intensity of the circumstances that caused him and Silas to leave Thessalonica. He saw in this more than resistance from the Jews or from the countrymen of the Thessalonians. He drew their attention to the spiritual aspect of these troubles due to the meddling of Satan. However, Paul noted how the work of Timothy reestablished contact with his readers, and how there was rejoicing in this celebration of Christian fellowship.

2:17 *torn away.* This refers to Paul's separation from the Thessalonians and the resultant deprivation. The past tense may point to a sudden separation due to persecution (Ac 17:10; see also 1:6 and note). In other contexts this verb means "made an orphan;" the apostle used it here in a figurative sense (along with the expressions "not in heart," "more eagerly," and "with great desire") to show how ardently he missed the Thessalonians. *for a short time.* Most likely

Paul wrote this Letter within a year after leaving Thessalonica. In the not too distant future he would return to Greece (Ac 20:2). *we endeavored the more eagerly . . . to see you face to face.* Paul did not provide details about these efforts, whether they involved resistance at the borders of Thessalonica or merely the hectic pace of following up with the many emerging congregations in Asia and Greece.

2:18 *come . . . again and again.* Visitation is not only necessary to these new believers at Thessalonica but also most needed in congregations today. Congregational members will benefit from regular visits by their pastor, elders, or other appointed leaders. Pastors and congregational leaders will benefit from visits by regional and national churchmen who can provide an objective look at what is happening in the congregation and with its priorities. Paul provided just such supervision to the congregations he planted and to those that came under his care. *Satan hindered us.* Satan uses human agents to bring obstacles before God's people. This may refer to the governing authorities of Thessalonica who sought to imprison Paul and Silas so they would not preach the Word (on personal, demonic "powers" using and even corrupting impersonal "powers" to try to accomplish their evil purposes, see the notes at Col 1:16; 2:15). However, the ultimate authority belonged to the Lord Jesus Christ and not to Satan (Mt 28:18). In view of this, Christians may confidently resist Satan's devices through prayer and redoubled efforts. Don't give up! Luther wrote,

> If you try to help yourself by your own thoughts and counsel, you will only make the matter worse and give the devil more space. For he has a serpent's head [Revelation 12:9]. If it finds an opening into which it can slip, the whole body will follow without stopping. But prayer can prevent him and drive him back. (LC III 111)

2:19 *crown of boasting.* Here (as often in the NT) the word "crown" refers to the garland awarded to the winner of an athletic competition (2Tm 2:5). This was not the golden, pointy crown we know from our storybook memories but a simple laurel wreath. Just as an athlete rejoices and boasts in a prize, so Paul would rejoice when he saw the Thessalonians before the Lord. Although the word "boasting" often refers to the sin of boasting, here is an example of the word being used in a favorable sense, of godly and justifiable pride in someone or something. *coming.* Paul lived in the present hope of seeing the living Christ once again, which contributed to his dedication in the face of hardship as well as the intensity of care that he showed to others such as the Thessalonians. *Is it not you?* Paul made the Thessalonians his prize. He did not seek to be first among the apostles in the Church's homeland, Jerusalem. He sought to be first in the hearts of the congregations he drew together on the frontiers of faith.

2:20 *glory*. The term refers to someone in whom another can take pride (see the imagery in 2:7, 11). What striking words! Would pastors and other congregational leaders today write so boldly that their members—who call them with problems and tears, who need to be gathered as sheep which stray—are indeed their treasured glory and joy? How easy it is to overlook what matters most in ministry and congregational life. Paul reminds us that it is the people that matter most.

3:1 *left behind . . . alone*. Paul very forcibly felt the deprivation of being alone; it is as though he is experiencing abandonment. Realizing that they cannot possibly return to the hostile situation they experienced, Paul devised other plans. *Athens*. This refers to the apostle's work recounted in Ac 17:15–34; this period of his life was a time of considerable difficulty for him. Athens was in Achaia, the southern province of the Greek Peninsula. Though Corinth was the capital of the province, Athens surpassed it as a cultural center. See map, p. xx.

3:2 *sent Timothy*. Paul and Silas sent young Timothy as their liaison since the angry Thessalonian citizens that attacked them would not recognize Timothy or his important mission. Consider Timothy's bravery in visiting a place so recently stirred by the proclamation of the Gospel. The Book of Acts does not report this episode of Timothy's ministry. Paul would not leave this new flock without a shepherd. *coworker*. God works through His servants (Jn 15:5; 1Co 3:9). Paul did not consider himself the sole dispenser of the Gospel of Jesus Christ. He recognized God's gifts and talents in others, such as Timothy (cf. Col 4:11), and willingly solicited their help. How much work of the kingdom might go undone if we made ourselves so indispensible that we could not let others help us? God not only gives us coworkers, He makes us coworkers so that we might together contribute to His kingdom goals. *establish and exhort*. Faith in Christ needs to be "rooted and built up in Him" (Col 2:7) by clinging to and erecting itself upon the Gospel promises. Faith is built up by the Word of God, so that through those who labor in the Word, the Lord builds our faith (Eph 4:15). Paul has in view the teaching of God's Word that deepens a person's understanding of what is good and right. With this he couples exhortation that drives deeper roots into the Word so that the hearers are not swayed by false teaching.

3:3 *afflictions.* The Thessalonians had been literally dragged before their city officials, suffering physically as well as emotionally (Ac 17:6–9). *destined.* What Paul wrote here may at first seem disturbing. The idea that Paul, Silas, and other children of God are destined to suffer may seem cruel, knowing that God has the power to overcome evil or to direct it away from us. Yet Paul is not suggesting that when Christians suffer they should simply accept that as their destiny without seeking relief or improvement. Consider the fact that Paul and Silas listened to their Thessalonian brethren who urged them to slip out of the city by night in order to preserve their lives and help. What Paul described was not a fatalistic martyr-mindset that seeks trouble or simply lies down under it. He reminded the Thessalonians that Christians are in the midst of a great spiritual conflict, which naturally brings trouble. Suffering for the sake of the Gospel is an intrinsic part of the Christian life. This is part of what Luther meant, when he spoke early in the Reformation of being a "theologian of the cross" (Heidelberg Disputation; LW 31:39–70). Neither the apostles nor our Lord Jesus promised that following Him would be easy (cf. Jn 16:33). On suffering and the Christian life, see the note at Col 1:24; see also Ac 14:21–22; Php 3:10; 2Tm 2:10.

3:4 *with you.* See the note at 2:1. *telling . . . beforehand.* It is not clear whether Paul anticipated the trouble due to his experiences in other places or whether this is an example of the apostle exercising his prophetic gifts. In either case, both he and the Thessalonian believers were prepared. *suffer affliction.* Paul and Silas narrowly escaped the mob that came after them in Thessalonica. When they were not found, the hosts (Jason and some other Christian brothers) were mistreated (Ac 17:5–9). *just as it has come to pass.* Paul emphasized the fulfillment of his message to them for, indeed, suffering is part of life "under the cross."

3:5 *sent.* Paul, being eager to know about his converts, sent Timothy, his helper. See note, v. 3. *tempter.* This is another reference to Satan (cf. 2:18). He used people and even other beings to derail disciples from their faith (cf. Gn 3:1–7). No doubt, the tempter continued his wicked work. Paul stopped short of voicing his full concern that the Thessalonians would yield to temptation and fall away from Christ.

3:6 *Timothy.* See the notes at 1:1 and 3:2. As Paul's representative, Timothy had spent an unspecified amount of time with the Thessalonians. *good news.* Here the term does not refer to the preaching of the Gospel but to the joyful news that the Thessalonians were well grounded in their faith in Christ and their love to others. Paul had earlier worried about them, not knowing whether they stood firm or fell from their faith in Christ due to the tempter (v. 5), Satan. *faith . . . love . . . long to see us.* Paul returned to the spiritual blessings and characteristics that he described in the lives of the Thessalonians at the opening of the letter. See note, 1:3.

3:7 *distress and affliction.* This letter was almost certainly written from Corinth in about 51 AD. That being the case, Ac 18:5–10 would give us an idea of the "distress and affliction" that the apostle and those with him were experiencing. (Luke reports a sharp exchange between Paul and Corinthian Jews who would not acknowledge Jesus as the Christ.) The two Greek words here, used together for emphasis, may also express the genuine Christian concern of Paul and his companions for their fellow believers (cf. Rm 12:15; 1Co 12:26).

3:8 *now we live.* How tightly he expressed the bond of pastoral care with them! This is a sincerely expressed rhetorical flourish for the sake of emphasis. Paul longed for their safety in the Gospel, as though his life depended on it. *standing fast in the Lord.* The Thessalonians were keeping true to the message of God's grace for the sake of Christ crucified. See note, v. 2.

3:9 *thanksgiving . . . return.* The apostle used a rhetorical question to express the awe and gratitude to God he was feeling after hearing about the faith of the Thessalonians. They certainly gave thanks and praise to God (1:2), yet realized that what they offered back to God was meager in comparison with the blessings He gave them through the Thessalonians, their crown (vv. 19–20).

3:10 *supply what is lacking in your faith?* Their trust in God was not defective or inadequate (see notes, 1:2–5). Rather, the Thessalonians needed instruction in certain matters as well as the continual nourishing and building up in the faith that all believers require throughout their time here on earth. Although Paul had earlier praised their faith, even the most mature believers may truthfully acknowledge how far they are from the fullness and perfection that God envisions for His beloved children. This is one of the reasons that a steady diet of Bible study and mutual prayer is so beneficial to every believer.

2:17–3:10 in Devotion and Prayer Paul was interested in the well-being of the Thessalonians and in learning whether they were standing firm in the Gospel or had yielded due to pressure from those who opposed them in the city. When Paul could no more bear the lack of news, he decided to send Timothy, his co-worker and helper, for Timothy could enter the city without being recognized by the opposition. Today, pastors and leaders in God's Church need to follow up on their members as well. They should take practical steps to know how they are, to encourage and exhort them to fulfill their faith despite affliction. The Lord seeks and wants to save and strengthen us through His servants, even in the midst of our problems. We are the apple of His eye. • Lord, give us Your loving heart, so that we may sincerely follow You and care for the flock You have put under our care. Lord, help us pass through the various sufferings that will come our way as we follow You. Amen.

Prayer (3:11–13)

ESV	KJV
[11]Now may our God and Father himself, and our Lord Jesus, direct our way to you, [12]and may the Lord make you increase and abound in love for one another and for all, as we do for you, [13]so that he may establish your hearts blameless in holiness before our God and Father, at the coming of our Lord Jesus with all his saints.	[11]Now God himself and our Father, and our Lord Jesus Christ, direct our way unto you. [12]And the Lord make you to increase and abound in love one toward another, and toward all men, even as we do toward you: [13]To the end he may stablish your hearts unblameable in holiness before God, even our Father, at the coming of our Lord Jesus Christ with all his saints.

Introduction to 3:11–13 After Paul had heard the encouraging report Timothy brought to him, he expressed his wishes for the

Thessalonians in a prayer of blessing for them. Paul stopped at any time to offer prayer to the Lord. He lived with a ready sense of God's presence. To the great apostle, God was not a distant, impersonal concept but a close and caring Lord who hears our cries and provides for us in Christ Jesus. Our hesitancy to pray is a dishonor to Him who stands ever near. Consider—He is present now and ready to hear you; therefore, pray.

3:11 God the Father and Christ are joint subjects of the sentence. The same function is ascribed to God the Father and to Jesus, who as the Second Person of the Trinity has divinity and equality with God the Father. On "Lord" as a designation for Jesus see the note at Col 1:3; on the divinity of Christ see the notes at Col 1:15; 2:9. *direct our way to you*. Although Paul was grateful for Timothy's report, he remained unsatisfied with anything less than a face to face visit (v. 10). He was counting on the Lord to direct His life toward this good goal. He made this a matter of prayer. Bengel wrote,

> Both epistles to the Thessalonians have almost all the several chapters singly sealed and distinguished by single breathings of prayer [each chapter sealed with its own prayer], 5:23; 2Th 1:11; 2:16; 3:5, 16. (Bengel 199)

3:12 *the Lord*. In commenting on the repetition of the divine title in these verses, Ambrose wrote: "Who, then, is the Lord. . . . He has named the Father and has named the Son; Whom, then, has he joined with the Father and the Son except the Spirit? Who is the Lord Who establishes our hearts in holiness" (*NPNF*2 10:149). Ambrose saw in this repetition an allusion to the Holy Trinity and the Holy Spirit's work of sanctification (cf. the work of the Spirit in 1:5–6). *increase and abound*. The increase spoken of here is a spiritual rather than a numerical one (cf. Eph 3:16). Genuine spiritual growth leads to outreach with the Gospel, which fosters congregational strength and also numerical growth. The love Paul described is outwardly focused first to one's fellow Christians but ultimately to all people, whom the Lord would save. *as we do for you*. Paul alluded to the earlier theme of imitation. See notes, 1:6; 2:14.

3:13 *establish your hearts*. In biblical vocabulary the "heart" designates the entirety of one's true, inner being and therefore refers to the mental and spiritual aspects of a person as well as the emotional aspect. Hence, this phrase is a prayer for the readers' stability that encompasses each one's entire existence. It is a prayer for spiritual wholeness. *blameless in holiness*. Holiness is the result of the Holy Spirit's work in a person's life through Word and Sacrament. The person thereby receives total forgiveness through faith in Christ, and being so forgiven, he is "blameless" before God. In Paul's teaching, love leads to the appropriate mutual care that causes peaceful relations between God's people. Later in his ministry, he would expound these thoughts in his Letter to the Romans. The latter half of that Letter, which focuses on the practical life of the congregation, is seasoned with teaching about the role of love in the Christian life (e.g., Rm 12:9–21; 13:8–10). This exercise of love leads to a life that others cannot condemn and may therefore be called "blameless." *coming of our Lord Jesus*. Although this phrase definitely refers to the second coming of Christ at the Day of Judgment, one should not fail also to point to the presence of the risen Lord among His people, His regular coming to them in His Word and Sacrament (on the power of God's Word, see the note at 1:5). As noted for v. 11, Paul lived with this sense that God's presence was here and now rather than distant. The Lord Jesus will presently direct them on the way that finally reaches His eternal throne. *with all His saints*. The Greek term for "saints" literally means "holy ones." Paul may refer to "the revealing of the sons of God" (Rm 8:19). In other words, deceased believers have been with the Lord in spirit (on which see the note at 5:10). When Christ will resurrect them bodily, He will gather them together with their fellow believers at His return in glory (see 1Th 4:16–17 and the notes there). However, "saints" or "holy ones" could here designate the angels who will accompany Christ at His second coming (Mk 8:38; 13:27; Rv 19:14). In the Parable of the Weeds (Mt 13:36–43) and the Parable of the Net (Mt 13:47–50), Jesus described the angels playing a very active role in the judgment. The judgment that accompanies the return of Jesus would certainly require established hearts that would recognize the blessedness of Christ's return rather than fear blame or lack of holiness. A third possibility is that the apostle may be deliberately writing inclusively, so as to cause the reader to think of both of the resurrected believers and the angels. In any case, the point of Paul's prayer is that they would be prepared to meet their Savior without fear.

3:11–13 in Devotion and Prayer Paul heard the good report from Timothy that the Thessalonians were standing in their faith and have the same kind of love for him as he has for them. His joy at this news moved him to a prayer of blessing for the Thessalonians, one that reached forward boldly to the time when Jesus will reappear. In view of Christ's return, our faith in the Lord and our accompanying love for one another should be as living and contagious as that of the Thessalonians. The Lord, who has promised to be with us until the end of time, will keep us in our faith in Him and kindle His love in our hearts so that we may love Him and one another. • We praise You, O God, because the gates of hell cannot prevent the sown seed of Your Word from growing. Direct our hearts humbly to call upon You and to serve one another with blameless love so that we may approach Your throne with boldness on that Last Day. Amen.

PART 2

EXHORTATIONS (4:1–5:22)

Introduction (4:1–2)

ESV	KJV
4 ¹Finally, then, brothers, we ask and urge you in the Lord Jesus, that as you received from us how you ought to walk and to please God, just as you are doing, that you do so more and more. ²For you know what instructions we gave you through the Lord Jesus.	4 ¹Furthermore then we beseech you, brethren, and exhort you by the Lord Jesus, that as ye have received of us how ye ought to walk and to please God, so ye would abound more and more. ²For ye know what commandments we gave you by the Lord Jesus.

Introduction to 4:1–12 Having praised the Thessalonians for the faith and example and having reviewed their progress, Paul then gave instruction on some practical matters dealing with the Christian's new life of sanctification (holy living). He did this with the specific intent that his readers' witness for the Lord may go forward blamelessly, as he prayed in 3:13. Paul commonly treated such matters in the latter part of his Letters after laying the theological foundation for Christian faith, love, and hope.

4:1 *Finally, then.* The imperatives of instruction that follow are based upon and empowered by the indicatives of salvation that the apostle has proclaimed in the previous chapters of this Letter. Paul sometimes used "finally" to introduce his section of instruction about life (see also Php 3:1; 2Th 3:1); in such passages it would perhaps be helpful to use a translation such as "therefore" or "furthermore" (so KJV) to distinguish this use of the word from those passages where it truly does introduce the apostle's closing point (e.g., 2Co 13:11). *in the Lord Jesus.* Cf. the expression "created in Christ Jesus for good works" in Eph 2:10; "in Christ" (see the note at Col 1:2) we are saved for good works and empowered to do those good works. Jesus is the source and sustainer of our faith, love, and hope. *how you ought to walk.* The Law is given as a guide for those who are already saved (this is sometimes called "the third use of the law," see FC, Ep and SD, VI). Paul gave a guideline to those already saved through faith in the Gospel of Jesus Christ. On the use of "walk" to describe the Christian life, see the notes at Col 1:10 and 2:6. *just as you are doing.* A phrase found in a number of early Greek manuscripts that did not appear in the majority of later Greek manuscripts, such as those upon which the KJV was based. *more and more.* An abundance of good works results from being grafted in Christ as a branch to the vine (Jn 15:4). A static Christian life, which does not remain active in faithful service, is in decline. That is not to say, however, that the Lord would drive us to be so busy that we make ourselves and everyone else miserable. The example of Jesus is helpful in this regard. Jesus served to the fullest and was certainly, with the apostles, driven to diligent ministry. Yet, we read several times in the Gospels about how Jesus withdrew from the needy crowds, especially to pray (Mk 1:35; 6:46; Lk 5:16; 6:12). God would have us recognize our limits and sustain our health and good attitude so that we have time and opportunity to truly abound "more and more."

4:2 *instructions.* The Lord taught Paul not only the truths of the Gospel but also what fruit the Gospel bears in a person's life. As a result, the Lord gives authority to Paul's instructions, which are also clearly rooted in Old Testament teaching. In this same year, or not too long afterward, Paul wrote to the Galatians his famous words about the "works of the flesh" and the "fruit of the Spirit" (Gal 5:10–24), which resemble points in the following verses.

On Marriage (4:3–8)

ESV	KJV
³For this is the will of God, your sanctification: that you abstain from sexual immorality; ⁴that each one of you know how to control his own body in holiness and honor, ⁵not in the passion of lust like the Gentiles who do not know God; ⁶that no one transgress and wrong his brother in this matter, because the Lord is an avenger in all these things, as we told you beforehand and solemnly warned you. ⁷For God has not called us for impurity, but in holiness. ⁸Therefore whoever disregards this, disregards not man but God, who gives his Holy Spirit to you.	³For this is the will of God, even your sanctification, that ye should abstain from fornication: ⁴That every one of you should know how to possess his vessel in sanctification and honour; ⁵Not in the lust of concupiscence, even as the Gentiles which know not God: ⁶That no man go beyond and defraud his brother in any matter: because that the Lord is the avenger of all such, as we also have forewarned you and testified. ⁷For God hath not called us unto uncleanness, but unto holiness. ⁸He therefore that despiseth, despiseth not man, but God, who hath also given unto us his holy Spirit.

4:3 *sanctification.* The same Greek word is rendered "holiness" in 3:13 (see note there). Through Christ's forgiveness, our relationship before God is "blameless in holiness." The Lord enables us to live a life of sanctification or holiness in thought, word, and deed. A person who has such a holy relationship with God must not continue to live in an unholy manner. A Christian's body is the temple of the Holy Spirit, who enables the believer to live a holy life (1Co 6:15–20). We are to be holy in our conduct, because God has made us holy by forgiving our unholiness through faith in Christ. *sexual immorality.* Paul began with this issue because of the notorious behaviors in the Gentile culture of that day. Behaviors that are not just frowned upon but illegal today were widely accepted in the Greek culture, which so strongly affected Macedonia, the homeland of the Thessalonians. The stories of Macedonia's greatest hero—Alexander the Great—suffice to illustrate the problems with sexual immorality. The Macedonians were especially devoted to the god Zeus, whose mythology is filled with stories of marital unfaithfulness.

4:4 *how to control his own body.* Our sexuality is God's gift to us. It will be for our good, if it is used exclusively within the parameters of marriage (Gn 1:27–28). The chief purpose of marriage is the bearing of children, who will in time inherit the family property and contribute to the good of the broader society. When these basic features of human life are out of control, family and society tend to decay, often rapidly so. For these reasons, every culture takes special pains to protect the bond of marriage so that appropriate laws safeguard this divine institution. Melanchthon concluded, "Good people will know how to control the use of marriage, especially when they occupy public offices" (Ap XXIII 43). Powerful public figures, in the church or the state, are not to abuse their status but are to set God-pleasing examples.

4:5 *like the Gentiles.* This refers to unbelievers outside of the Church. Paul could make this blanket statement about such people living by gratifying their lustful passions in wanton self-indulgence, as lax sexual conduct was almost universal in the first century Greco-Roman world. Sexual infidelity was nearly expected from men. Christianity was radically different because it taught that a man should be faithful to his wife by not having sex with other persons. *do not know God.* When people do not know the true God, they are more likely to behave according to their destructive and self-destructive passions. Here "know" refers not to mere intellectual knowledge but to having an actual relationship with God (much as the OT could use the verb "know" to refer to intimate relations; e.g., Gn 4:1). Humans have an inherent sense that God exists (Rm 1:19–20), yet they sinfully corrupt that knowledge into idolatry (Rm 1:21–23), so that they do not "know" God in the sense of having a genuine faith relationship with Him.

4:6 *wrong his brother.* The phrase means wronging another person by having an intimate sexual relationship with him/her or by taking advantage of another person's spouse or family members. Adultery and fornication harm another person by making use of what God, the Creator of our sexuality, intends to be reserved solely for one's spouse. Thus, to engage in sex outside of marriage is to do harm to yourself, to the other person, to your spouse, your family, and to the other person's spouse and family. Worldly views of sexuality conclude that, so long as no one is harmed, "romantic" affairs are tolerable or even to be preferred. Remarkably, modern moral philosophers delight in referring to the sexual behaviors of animals as a basis for guiding human behavior. They conclude that since human beings evolved from animals that do not practice marital faithfulness, therefore, unfaithfulness is the "natural" state of human sexual behavior. In other words human reason knows no boundaries for justifying self-indulgence! *avenger*. Jealousy and wrath are the common outcomes of unfaithfulness and even flirtatious behavior. A part of the reason that society wishes to govern marital and sexual relations is because violations of these bonds so often lead to violence. The Bible goes a step further: the anger and wrath of the holy and jealous God will be on those who have not repented of their sin and are not covered by the blood of His Son (Eph 5:6; Col 3:5–6). Paul warned elsewhere that "the wages of sin is death" (Rm 6:23). If the jealous spouse or family member does not pursue the one practicing sexual immorality, the Creator will at the very least leave him to the consequences of his wickedness (Rm 1:28–32). *beforehand*. This shows that Paul taught about these matters while carrying out his ministry in Thessalonica (Ac 17:1–9); this indicates that instruction about such matters would have been a regular part of the apostle's teaching in the churches that he formed.

4:7 *called us.* God called us to saving faith through the Gospel of Christ alone (e.g., 2Th 2:14). Yet as a consequence of this, He has also called us to holy living ("sanctification"). The children of God are to resemble their holy, heavenly Father. Christians need to see their lives in this respect: the call to salvation includes a call to honor the Savior in one's life.

4:8 *gives His Holy Spirit.* Our reception of the Holy Spirit is not our achievement. The Holy Spirit is given when the Word about Christ and His Sacraments are received by faith. The Holy Spirit reveals the meaning of the Word and the Sacraments by testifying to Christ. In this way the Holy Spirit makes us holy before God through faith in Christ and thereby enables us to lead holy lives. *to you.* The KJV and other older translations have "to us," which harmonizes with "us" in v. 7. The ESV chooses an early, though weakly represented reading that harmonizes better with the "you" of v. 6. In either case, Paul applied his teaching to the Thessalonians.

On Brotherly Love and Self-Sufficiency (4:9–12)

ESV	KJV
[9]Now concerning brotherly love you have no need for anyone to write to you, for you yourselves have been taught by God to love one another, [10]for that indeed is what you are doing to all the brothers throughout Macedonia. But we urge you, brothers, to do this more and more, [11]and to aspire to live quietly, and to mind your own affairs, and to work with your hands, as we instructed you, [12]so that you may walk properly before outsiders and be dependent on no one.	[9]But as touching brotherly love ye need not that I write unto you: for ye yourselves are taught of God to love one another. [10]And indeed ye do it toward all the brethren which are in all Macedonia: but we beseech you, brethren, that ye increase more and more; [11]And that ye study to be quiet, and to do your own business, and to work with your own hands, as we commanded you; [12]That ye may walk honestly toward them that are without, and that ye may have lack of nothing.

4:9 *brotherly love.* On the family aspect of churchly life, see note Col 1:2. *taught by God.* What Paul taught the Thessalonians did not consist of his own ideas. The apostle taught the Word of God, through which the Holy Spirit Himself taught them (cf. Jn 14:26; 16:13). To be taught by God is not only to be informed by Him but to be transformed in faith and life (cf. Rm 12:1). Try this thought on for a moment. After leaving your Bible study or devotion, consider telling the next person you speak with, "God taught me something today" and share what you have learned. *love one another.* On the night when Jesus was betrayed, knowing what was about to take place and how the disciples would be scared and scattered, He placed tremendous emphasis on this teaching (Jn 13:31–35). The Lord taught this also to the Thessalonians while they were facing the tensions of persecution in their city. On a different note, how striking is this teaching of brotherly love from Jesus compared with the all-too-common perversion of love against which Paul admonished them in vv. 3–6. Today one can hardly use the word "love" without people thinking of sex, since we have become so Freudian in our thinking. Lord, have mercy and teach us again the purity and value of brotherly love.

4:10 *Macedonia.* See the notes at 1:1; 1:7. This would have involved, at a minimum, the churches at Philippi and Berea (Ac 16:6–40;

17:10–15). Paul indicated that congregations or individual Christians existed not just in Thessalonica but at other places in Macedonia.

4:11 *aspire to live quietly.* Paul showed that Christians need to put limits on how they interact with others. The Christian life is balanced. The term "quietly" would seem to imply not being overly concerned with worldly matters (cf. 2Th 3:12) that draw one into the limelight or into open conflict with one's neighbors. Since the Greek word used here sometimes means to stop speaking (Lk 14:4; Ac 11:18; 21:14), this passage would also indicate that the believer must learn when to speak (see the note at Col 4:3) and when to keep silent (Ec 3:7b). *mind your own affairs.* We might say, "mind your own business." The apostle's instruction is in keeping with biblical injunctions against gossip and busybodies (2Th 3:11; see also Rm 1:29; 2Co 12:20; 1Tm 5:13). Luther put it this way:

> It is not only necessary for our life that our body have food and clothes and other necessaries. It is also necessary that we spend our days in peace and quiet among the people with whom we live and have dealings in daily business and conversation and all sorts of doings. (LC III 73)

However, readers should be careful not to add to this admonition from Paul the idea that Christians should simply live as "silent witnesses" who do not need to speak of Jesus Christ with their neighbors, family, or acquaintances. Paul clearly did just that—he spoke up repeatedly and all around the Mediterranean! Christians are decidedly called to speak the Gospel boldly, and Paul praised the Thessalonians for doing so (1:8). Nevertheless, when sharing the faith brings persecution, as happened in Thessalonica (Ac 17), Paul did not urge them to press on to martyrdom but to work for peace that gives the opportunity for the Gospel to be sown, to sprout, and to grow. *work with your hands.* Earn your living from your own labor. Christian generosity and kindness can produce the unwanted effect of making perfectly healthy or capable people dependent upon others instead of inspiring them to "pull their own weight," as we say. Here is another matter of balance: knowing when to give and knowing when to say to someone, "It is time for you to manage your own affairs." *as we instructed you.* See notes, 2:15; 4:9; Col 2:7. Paul and Silvanus themselves set a good example for the Thessalonians by earning their living when they stayed and ministered among them (2:9).

4:12 *walk properly.* See note, 2:12. *outsiders.* Paul had unbelievers in mind; see further 1Co 14:16–17. *dependent on no one.* Paul urged them to live on the fruits of their physical labor. Work is not a curse but a blessing in biblical thinking. This is readily seen from the history of God's creation when He made Adam and Eve to take care of the Garden of Eden (Gn 2:15). God Himself worked during the process of creation (Gn 2:3). Work only became onerous after the fall into sin (Gn 3:17–19). God designed us to work and intended it for our good. From this passage and 2Th 3:10–12 it also appears that some in Thessalonica had ceased working, so that others had to provide for them. This situation seems to have arisen from mistaken ideas about the second coming of Christ (2Th 2:2); hence, the apostle immediately followed this section with his teaching on the return of Christ (4:13–5:11).

4:1–12 in Devotion and Prayer In this section, Paul gives advice on some practical matters dealing with sanctification, so that his readers' witness for the Lord may go forward blamelessly. He especially emphasizes the role of brotherly love and the need for balance in the Christian life and witness as we await the Lord's reappearing. We Christians must lead a sexually pure life so that we may not grieve the Holy Spirit. Our love to one another should not be superficial but honest and from the heart. We should live by our labor without improperly depending on others for support. The Lord—through His Spirit poured upon us—fights for us against the "flaming darts of the evil one" (Eph 6:16) so that we may live pure and blameless lives. • "Finish then Thy new creation, Pure and spotless let us be; Let us see Thy great salvation Perfectly restored in Thee, Changes from glory into glory, Till in heav'n we take our place, Till we cast our crowns before Thee, Lost in wonder, love, and praise!" Amen. (*LSB* 700:4; *H82* 657:3; *TPH* 376:4; *TUMH* 384:4)

On Clarifying Concerns about the End Times (4:13–5:11)

Those who have fallen asleep (4:13–18)

ESV	KJV
[13]But we do not want you to be uninformed, brothers, about those who are asleep, that you may not grieve as others do who have no hope. [14]For since we believe that Jesus died and rose again, even so, through Jesus, God will bring with him those who have fallen asleep. [15]For this we declare to you by a word from the Lord, that we who are alive, who are left until the coming of the Lord, will not precede those who have fallen asleep. [16]For the Lord himself will descend from heaven with a cry of command, with the voice of an archangel, and with the sound of the trumpet of God. And the dead in Christ will rise first. [17]Then we who are alive, who are left, will be caught up together with them in the clouds to meet the Lord in the air, and so we will always be with the Lord. [18]Therefore encourage one another with these words.	[13]But I would not have you to be ignorant, brethren, concerning them which are asleep, that ye sorrow not, even as others which have no hope. [14]For if we believe that Jesus died and rose again, even so them also which sleep in Jesus will God bring with him. [15]For this we say unto you by the word of the Lord, that we which are alive and remain unto the coming of the Lord shall not prevent them which are asleep. [16]For the Lord himself shall descend from heaven with a shout, with the voice of the archangel, and with the trump of God: and the dead in Christ shall rise first: [17]Then we which are alive and remain shall be caught up together with them in the clouds, to meet the Lord in the air: and so shall we ever be with the Lord. [18]Wherefore comfort one another with these words.

Introduction to 4:13–18 Now Paul comes to one of the most important reasons for him to write to the congregation. Although, as he indicated earlier, he hoped to encourage the congregation generally and "supply what is lacking" in their faith generally, the report from Timothy must have made him aware of this special need. In this section and the following section Paul wrote at length about the reappearing of Christ (Greek *parousia*, "presence" or "coming" in 4:15). All indications are that this was a topic of special interest at Thessalonica and that there were some misunderstandings about it held by at least some of the believers there. Having strengthened the bond with the Thessalonians in the first four chapters, he then dealt directly with this misunderstanding in a gentle way. This is one of the most encouraging portions of all of Scripture for those mourning the death of a fellow believer.

4:13 *asleep.* This is a common biblical euphemism for death (cf. 1Ki 2:10). In other words, it is a gentle or polite way of speaking about something painful. Some worldly euphemisms for death (e.g., "no longer with us") attempt to avoid the awful reality of death by making no reference to it. Paul acknowledged death in all its horror (e.g., he spoke of the "dead in Christ" in v. 16; cf. also death as an enemy in 1Co 15:26). However, along with other writers of the Scripture, Paul called death a sleep in bold recognition of the truth that Christ's resurrection has made our physical death something temporary. For Christ will awaken believers bodily at the final resurrection. A modern error to avoid for this topic is the idea of "soul sleep," which holds that the souls of believers sleep with their bodies until the resurrection. Various NT passages plainly indicate that the soul is alert after death, either facing the punishment of hell or enjoying eternal life in the bliss of Christ's presence (Mt 22:32; Lk 16:19–31; Php 1:21–24; Heb 12:22–24; Rv 6:9–11; 19:1; cf. Paul's experience in 2Co 12:2). Even the OT gives examples of persons who went to be with the Lord without any record of them having to pass through a stage of sleep (Enoch, Gn 5:24; Elijah, 2Ki 2:11). *grieve.* Christians will still grieve at the death of a fellow believer, but they will do so in a different manner than will those who have no hope. The fact that Christ is risen from the dead provides a greater comfort than any other. No Christian funeral should pass without reading promises of the resurrection from Scripture and proclaiming this comforting promise for those who sorrow. Bengel wrote, "The Scripture, from among so many topics of consolation in regard to death, generally brings forward this one concerning the resurrection, as principal and pre-eminent" (Bengel 202). *others.* The apostle was referring to all those who do not know God through true faith in Christ. For many today, death is an end with no thought of the future. Some philosophies counsel people to make peace with death, neither understanding that death is an enemy to God's gift of life nor the gift of eternal life received through faith. At most, they try to strain some comfort from the idea that once someone is dead, nothing further can afflict him. Once, a troubled man reflected on the death of his father while sitting in the pastor's office. He tried to console himself with the idea that death is the end, after which nothing either good or bad happens to a person. The man's comments confused the pastor who learned only later that the man was planning to leave his wife for another woman. Under these guilt ridden circumstances, the idea of hiding guilt-free in the grave was somehow comforting to him! But the grave is no foxhole for sinners. Lord, have mercy. *no hope.* Those who live without Jesus have no hope because they do not know of or trust in the resurrection (cf. Eph 2:12). The general lack of hope in the ancient world is attested by these lines from the Greek tragedy *Oedipus Coloneus* (lines 1225–26): "Not to be born at all—that is by far the best fortune; and the second best is as soon as one is born with all speed to return thither whence one has come." Given these thoughts, one can see why Paul's message of the resurrection was both scorned by some Greeks (Ac 17:32) as well as eagerly welcomed by others such as the Thessalonians.

4:14 *rose.* This is the sole place in the apostle's Letters where he referred to the resurrection of Christ as something that Christ did. Elsewhere Scripture records that God the Father or the Holy Spirit raised Jesus (e.g., Ac 2:24, 32; Rm 6:4; 8:11). In view of this, one may properly regard the resurrection as a miracle of the Holy Trinity, as each person actively participated in this cornerstone of our faith. In a similar way, all three persons of the Trinity will participate in our bodily resurrection on the Last Day. *bring with Him.* Jesus will be a mediator through whom the dead are resurrected (on the role of God the Holy Spirit in the resurrection, see Rm 1:4; 8:11).

4:15 *by a word from the Lord.* Paul then referred either to a teaching of our Lord Jesus Christ (e.g., Mt 22:23–33) or to a revelation given to the apostles in Jesus' name. The Holy Spirit actively inspired the writings of the apostles, which we have in the NT. However, He also inspired their preaching and teaching, sometimes providing prophetic insight to them as they ministered (e.g., Ac 18:9–10). *we who are alive.* At this point Paul may have thought that he would still be alive at the second coming. However, he did not teach that Jesus would certainly reappear during his own lifetime (1Co 6:14; Php 1:21–23; 2Tm 4:6). *precede.* Due to the resurrection of the body, those who died in Christ will lack no advantage when the Lord returns. They will see and experience the second coming just as the living will. Paul was apparently refuting a point or a question that someone had raised about the resurrection. We know from 2Th 2:2 that at some time the Thessalonians had received a letter that confused them about the end times. Calvin wrote,

> Ordinary death, it is true, is the separation of the soul from the body; but this does not hinder that the Lord may in a moment destroy this corruptible nature, so as to create it anew by his power, for thus is accomplished what Paul himself teaches must take place—that mortality shall be swallowed up of life. (2 Cor. 5:4.) (Calvin 283)

4:16 *cry . . . voice . . . sound.* These terms are three ways of expressing the same action (calling) of the Lord. *command.* This refers to the quickening Word of the Lord (cf. Jn 5:28–29). At the beginning of creation, the Lord brought forth life by a simple command (Gn 1:20, 24, 26). The miracle is echoed in the new creation as the Word of life sounds forth (Jn 1:1–4; Php 2:16). Consider also the story of Lazarus, who though dead in the tomb for four days, promptly came forth when Jesus called him. What a shocking experience that must have been for those who gathered at the tomb! Imagine how much more shocking will be that day when millions like Lazarus hear Jesus' voice and emerge from the earth. The Early Church father John Chrysostom wrote:

> When they see the earth agitated, the dust mingling, the bodies rising perchance on every side, no one [causing] this, but the 'shout' being sufficient . . . when they see so great a tumult upon the earth,—then they shall know. . . . What fear will possess those that remain upon the earth. (*NPNF*1 13:356)

voice of an archangel. The word "archangel" is used only one other time in the NT (Jude 9), with reference to Michael, the chief of the angels (cf. Dn 10:13; 12:1; Rv 12:7). The Lord uses angels to execute His will, and they are to accompany Him at His return (Mt 25:31; see note, 3:13). Hence, this passage fits in perfectly with what we know of angels from the rest of Scripture. The pseudepigraphical book 1 Enoch mentioned seven archangels: Uriel, Raphael, Raguel, Michael, Sarakiel, Gabriel, and Remiel (1Enoch 20:1–7). *trumpet.* A similar statement is found in Mt 24:30–31; 1Co 15:52. In the LXX, this Greek word most often translates the word for a ram's horn, which was not used as a musical instrument. Ancient Israelites used such trumpets to call people to meetings, such as gathering for worship, and to convey orders to troops. Shepherds might even use them for gathering their flocks, which provides us with a beautiful image of our Good Shepherd on that Last Day. Though He comes to earth in judgment, He comes in blessing for His little lambs, who hear and heed His voice (Jn 10:3, 16, 27). *dead in Christ*. Those who passed away while believing in the Lord will rise first from the grave before being taken to heaven (cf. v. 15).

4:17 Cf. 2Th 1:5–10. *who are left*. This refers to believers who are alive on the earth at the time of the Lord's reappearing. *caught up*. The Greek term is *harpazo*; it carries with it the sense of a sudden and violent action. The point is that we will be gathered together at the resurrection, the dead as well as the living, when Christ returns. The Vulgate translated *harpazo* with the Latin term *raptus*. This is the word from which the modern false doctrine of a "rapture," first proposed in the early 19th century, gets its name. Paul's teaching is about the resurrection and not a secret return of Christ—the so-called "rapture." Consider the following truths: (1) There will be a single bodily resurrection of the believing and the unbelieving (Ac 24:14–15). (2) There will be only one more reappearing of Christ after His earthly ministry in the first century AD (Heb 9:27–28). (3) This bodily resurrection and the reappearing of Christ will take place at the same time (1Co 15:23). (4) Scripture teaches that this all will take place at the Last Day (Jn 6:39–40). *meet the Lord in the air*. In the ancient world, dignitaries were welcomed officially by people who escorted them. The focus here is the coming together of the Lord and His people. The air is considered to be the abode of evil spirits (Eph 2:2), yet these will yield the place to Him who has all authority in the heavens and on earth. *always be with the Lord*. This describes life in heaven after the resurrection. Before the resurrection of the body, the souls of those who were in Christ dwelt with the Lord (see note, v. 13). However, after the resurrection, the bodies will be united again with the souls and believers will dwell in heaven wholly renewed.

4:18 *encourage one another*. The Thessalonians' concern, which prompted Paul's comments, is not entirely clear to us. Some Thessalonians may have feared that loved ones who had died in Christ might not be able to see the second coming of the Lord. Paul's teaching here encouraged them by correcting such a mistaken notion about those "who are asleep" (4:14). The word translated here as "encourage" is something more than a mere pep talk. Rather, it carries the idea that the message spoken ("with these words") will really build up the one who hears. Paul used this term numerous times in writing to the Thessalonians (1Th 2:12; 3:2, 7; 4:1, 10, 18; 5:11, 14; 2Th 2:17; 3:12) to express thoughts of urging, exhorting, and comforting. The word is also famously used to title the Holy Spirit as "the Comforter" (KJV in Jn 14:16). Some even use the Greek word itself, calling the Holy Spirit "the Paraclete." All of this helps to characterize this Letter of Paul, one of his earliest preserved in the NT, as a letter of encouragement or exhortation.

4:13–18 in Devotion and Prayer Paul comforts the Thessalonians, saying that the dead in Christ will be the first to taste the resurrection and come with the risen Christ. At the second coming, we will all be together once more. Today, Christians grieve over the death of loved ones, but not as those who have no hope. The resurrection of our Lord, and the victory we have over death through Him, gives us a living hope, despite the fact that death separates loved ones and causes great pain. Ironically, our technology today is used to prolong our lives. Yet at the same time, it allows us to gather more and more news from afar and amass a most discouraging series of news reports about death, murder, disasters, and other horrors. This includes the news that more Christians have suffered death for the faith in the last 100 years than at any other time in history. Now more than ever we need the Good News from our Good Shepherd, whose encouraging word delivers us from evil and from worry. We pray earnestly for the comfort of His Holy Spirit and await eagerly the promised resurrection of the body and the life everlasting with Him.
• "My flesh in hope shall rest And for a season slumber Till trump from east to west Shall wake the dead in number: Had Christ, who once was slain, Not burst His three-day prison, Our faith had been in vain: But now has Christ arisen, arisen, arisen; But now has Christ arisen!" (*LSB* 482:3)

The coming of the day of the Lord (5:1–11)

ESV	KJV
5 ¹Now concerning the times and the seasons, brothers, you have no need to have anything written to you. ²For you yourselves are fully aware that the day of the Lord will come like a thief in the night. ³While people are saying, "There is peace and security," then sudden destruction will come upon them as labor pains come upon a pregnant woman, and they will not escape. ⁴But you are not in darkness, brothers, for that day to surprise you like a thief. ⁵For you are all children of light, children of the day. We are not of the night or of the darkness. ⁶So then let us not sleep, as others do, but let us keep awake and be sober. ⁷For those who sleep, sleep at night, and those who get drunk, are drunk at night. ⁸But since we belong to the day, let us be sober, having put on the breastplate of faith and love, and for a helmet the hope of salvation. ⁹For God has not destined us for wrath, but to obtain salvation through our Lord Jesus Christ, ¹⁰who died for us so that whether we are awake or asleep we might live with him. ¹¹Therefore encourage one another and build one another up, just as you are doing.	5 ¹But of the times and the seasons, brethren, ye have no need that I write unto you. ²For yourselves know perfectly that the day of the Lord so cometh as a thief in the night. ³For when they shall say, Peace and safety; then sudden destruction cometh upon them, as travail upon a woman with child; and they shall not escape. ⁴But ye, brethren, are not in darkness, that that day should overtake you as a thief. ⁵Ye are all the children of light, and the children of the day: we are not of the night, nor of darkness. ⁶Therefore let us not sleep, as do others; but let us watch and be sober. ⁷For they that sleep sleep in the night; and they that be drunken are drunken in the night. ⁸But let us, who are of the day, be sober, putting on the breastplate of faith and love; and for an helmet, the hope of salvation. ⁹For God hath not appointed us to wrath, but to obtain salvation by our Lord Jesus Christ, ¹⁰Who died for us, that, whether we wake or sleep, we should live together with him. ¹¹Wherefore comfort yourselves together, and edify one another, even as also ye do.

Introduction to 5:1–11 After the previous section's description of the future glory of those who have died in Christ, Paul then proceeded to tell the Thessalonians about the coming Day of Judgment in which the Lord will give His final verdict. The apostle instructed his readers, so that they might always be prepared for the coming of that great day. (His words seem almost like a commentary on Jesus' teaching as recorded in Lk 21:34–36 and other places.) The seriousness of Paul's charge to them was conveyed by comparisons about standing guard, sobriety, and putting on a soldier's armor. As we saw earlier, Paul wished to comfort and encourage his readers, but he also did not wish to lull them into complacency. He likewise returned to the themes of faith, love, and hope with which he began to write (cf. 1:3; 5:8).

5:1 The Greek word translated here as "time" (*chronos*) referred to stretches of time, whereas the word rendered "seasons" (*kairos*) referred to a point in time, in the sense of "the right time." Paul used both terms here without any great distinction between them; rather, he was saying that he did not need to write to the Thessalonians anything pertaining to the time of the second coming beyond what they had already been taught (v. 2). Pairing these Greek terms seems to have formed a common expression. See Ac 1:7.

5:2 *day of the Lord.* In the OT, this referred to the Day of Judgment, in which the righteous will be vindicated and Yahweh ("the Lord") will make an impartial judgment. In the NT, with the recognition of Jesus as "Lord" (the equivalent of the divine name "Yahweh" from the OT), the function of final judgment is attributed to Jesus. Therefore, here "the day of the Lord" refers to the day in which Christ will be revealed in glory to vindicate His people and to judge the world in righteousness. For further study of the OT background and its influence on the NT, see Am 5:18–20; Jl 1:15; 2:31; Zph 1:14–16; Php 1:6–11; 2Th 2:1–2; 2Pt 3:10–12. *like a thief in the night.* This surprising expression grew even more surprising in the Book of Revelation where Jesus described Himself "like a thief" (Rv 3:3; 16:15), which may at first seem inappropriate to some devout souls. But the careful reader will not miss the point the biblical writers wish to record with such comparisons. The Lord's coming will be sudden (v. 3) and unexpected (Mt 24:36); cf. Lk 12:39. It is important to be alert, looking forward to the Lord's coming. We ought not to drop our guard like the man who went down to Jericho and fell among robbers (Lk 10:30). Instead, the Lord calls us to be watchmen, prepared for His appearing, and living with Good Samaritan readiness (Lk 10:30–37).

5:3 *sudden.* The end will come without warning (Lk 21:34–35) and all at once (1Co 15:52). Paul put words on the lips of the lax who only anticipated peace, as though the world would go on as usual. This is precisely the opposite of the watchman's attitude, who does not wish to be distracted from the Lord's purposes. *destruction.* This term denotes utter and hopeless ruin and despair (punishment, not annihilation, see e.g., Mk 9:48) for those who put their hope in this world rather than in Christ. The great medieval preacher, Bernard of Clairvaux, wrote: "Do not, while present prosperity smiles upon you, forget its certain end, lest adversity without end succeed it" (*SLSB*, p 56). Although the diligence of faith, love, and hope in this life may seem too zealous to many, they do not perceive how small such efforts are when compared to the eternity that God sees. We are like the disciples whom Jesus invited to "Watch with Me" on the night in which He was betrayed. They could not stay alert one hour (Mt 26:38–41) and we, too, are in danger of drifting off even as the footsteps of doom march forth. *labor pains.* The point of this comparison seems to be that the coming of these things is inevitable. As so often happens with a pregnancy, there are reoccurring signs that the moment of birth is to come. False labor will give way to real labor. Although the precise moment may remain unknown, it will definitely arrive. *escape.* By human reason and strength, no one can escape God's righteous judgment and scrutiny (Ps 139:7–10). Only those sheltered in Christ will escape God's wrath, which will come upon all those who have broken His righteous Law.

5:4–5 *day . . . night.* These terms are used figuratively here. As people walk in the light of the sun, and so are able to move in safety and security, so all those who walk in the light of the Word of God, Jesus Christ, have the security of His salvation. For further study on "light" and "darkness" as theological concepts, see Jn 1:4–9; 3:19–21; 8:12; 12:35–36; Eph 5:8–14.

5:6 *sleep.* Here the term does not refer to death (see note at 4:13) but to a life in sin and unbelief, which is a life in darkness. In contrast, those in Christ, the light of the world, are awake and sober and hence always prepared for the coming of the Day of the Lord. Roman soldiers who kept the night watch were expected to stay fully alert even under the most difficult conditions. If they failed to stay awake, the penalty could be death. Even today, codes of military justice include such harsh penalties for drunken or sleeping sentries during war time. This is because the security of the whole camp depends at night on those few individuals to stand at the edge, watch, and peer out into the darkness. Cf. Paul's words to the Romans in 13:11–14.

5:7 This is the commonsense basis of the figurative language that the apostle used above.

5:8 *breastplate . . . helmet.* The military language used here is based on the Roman army, familiar to NT believers, and especially on the description of the divine warrior in Is 59:17. See also in the Apocrypha, Wis 5:17–20. (These same sources help form the background to the fuller military imagery used in Eph 6:10–17, which see.) Paul advised the Thessalonians to guard their faith and love in Christ and His promises in the Gospel of the salvation to come, so that they would withstand all kinds of spiritual assaults. *hope.* See the notes at Col 1:5 and 1Th 4:13.

5:9 *destined.* God's purpose is the salvation of all people (1Tm 2:4). He does not want anyone to be lost. The faith active among the Thessalonians was the proof that He destined them for salvation. See further the notes at 2Th 2:13, 14. The early Christian bishop of Constantinople, John Chrysostom, wrote:

> Do not despair of yourself, O man, in going to God, who has not spared even His Son for you. Faint not at present evils. . . . Neither should we fear, if we were going to a judge who was about to judge us, and who had shown so much love for us, as to have sacrificed his son. Let us hope therefore for kind and great things. (*NPNF*1 13:363)

5:10 *died for us.* Christ died as our substitute. As the blameless and holy Son of God, He did not deserve to die. But out of love for us, He who was holy died on our behalf so that we may be free from the wrath of God that we deserved on account of our sin (2Co 5:21). After paying the debt of our sin, He rose from death. Based on the military comparisons Paul used, one might think of a private struggling to keep watch on duty and failing to stay alert. The other sentries find him asleep and the military police take him away. At the soldier's trial, he is condemned only to have the commander of his unit—indeed, the supreme commander—take his penalty. *awake or asleep.* This means, whether we are physically dead or still alive, we will have eternal life with Him (see the note at 4:13). The apostle wrote here of believers living with Christ even while asleep in death and prior to the resurrection at the Last Day (the resurrection at the

Last Day is the subject of 4:16–17). This life with Christ between the time of the believer's death and his resurrection at the Lord's return is known as the "intermediate state." See further Lk 23:43; 2Co 5:6–8; Php 1:21–24. See also note, 4:13.

5:11 *build one another up.* The Thessalonians can help one another grow spiritually (see 2Th 1:3 and note); this term adds to our understanding of the meaning of "encourage;" see the note at 4:18. Luther referred to such encouraging and building up of one another as "the mutual conversation and consolation of brethren" (SA III iv).

5:1–11 in Devotion and Prayer Let us walk in holiness and righteousness so that we may not be ashamed when our Lord appears as judge of the living and the dead. The Lord who has chosen us for salvation and died for us will be on our side on the final Day of Judgment. In view of this, we may live confidently as children of the light who are sober, alert, and armed against the works of darkness. • "May Christ our intercessor be And through His blood and merit Read from His book that we are free With all who life inherit. Then we shall see Him face to face, With all His saints in that blest place Which He has purchased for us." Amen. (*LSB* 508:6)

On Life in the Congregation (5:12–22)

Pastoral care among the congregation (5:12–15)

ESV	KJV
¹²We ask you, brothers, to respect those who labor among you and are over you in the Lord and admonish you, ¹³and to esteem them very highly in love because of their work. Be at peace among yourselves. ¹⁴And we urge you, brothers, admonish the idle, encourage the fainthearted, help the weak, be patient with them all. ¹⁵See that no one repays anyone evil for evil, but always seek to do good to one another and to everyone.	¹²And we beseech you, brethren, to know them which labour among you, and are over you in the Lord, and admonish you; ¹³And to esteem them very highly in love for their work's sake. And be at peace among yourselves. ¹⁴Now we exhort you, brethren, warn them that are unruly, comfort the feebleminded, support the weak, be patient toward all men. ¹⁵See that none render evil for evil unto any man; but ever follow that which is good, both among yourselves, and to all men.

Introduction to 5:12–15 Paul gave instruction about leadership within the Christian congregation. These verses contribute greatly to the biblical presentation of the office of the pastoral ministry and to how life should be within the Church. Paul established offices of leadership within the Thessalonian congregation as well as the calling of the general membership to admonish and encourage one another.

5:12 *those over you in the Lord and admonish you.* Compare what is said here to what is written about the "leaders" of Heb 13:7, 17. These leaders were "over" the other believers in that they provided spiritual "oversight," as did the "overseers" of 1Tm 3:1 and Ti 1:7. Although no official designation or title is applied to these leaders in Thessalonica, their duties are the same as those called "overseers," "elders," and "pastors/shepherds" elsewhere in the NT (Ac 20:28; Eph 4:11–13; 1Tm 3:1–7; Ti 1:5–9). Hence, this verse and the following one help inform our understanding of what the pastoral office should be. Wesley wrote,

> O what a misery it is when a man undertakes this whole work, without either gifts or graces for any part of it! Why then will he undertake it? For pay? What! Will he sell both his own soul, and all the souls of the flock? What words can describe such a wretch as this? (Wesley 531)

5:13 *esteem.* What is owed to these leaders is similar to what the recipients of the Letter to the Hebrews were instructed to give to those who "spoke to (them) the word of God" (13:7, 17). *their work.* These leaders/pastors were to be honored because of their service in the spirit of Christ's teaching (cf. Mt 23:11).

5:14 *admonish the idle.* Note that the task of reproving those who neglect their daily duty of work and live on the support of others is not only the responsibility of the leaders (pastors) but of the whole community of believers. Do not pass too quickly over this important point. The laity of the Christian congregation are not to be idle, nor are they silent, passive followers of the called ministers of the Word. The laity are to voice the Word and are to serve with diligence. On the problem of idleness among the Christians at Thessalonica, see 2Th 3:6–12 and the notes there. *idle . . . fainthearted . . . weak.* Congregations consist of different groups of people. People at differing levels of growth in faith and in Christian living need appropriately different treatment from their pastor(s) and other fellow Christians.

be patient. Patience is part of the fruit of the Spirit (Gal 5:22) and it is manifested in love toward others: "Love is patient" (1Co 13:4). A Christian shows love not only to the strong but also to the weak and the fainthearted.

5:15 *evil for evil.* The natural instinct of most people is to hurt someone who has hurt them. One does not need to be a police officer or professional psychologist to learn this. Only spend a little time at a playground observing children and you will soon see how natural it is for people to lash back at others when they believe they were treated unfairly. Paul sought to steer the congregation away from this playground, street-justice mentality. Drawing on the teachings of Jesus, he taught something far higher and difficult to live by. *seek to do good.* This admonition from Paul is deceptively simple. On first reading, one might conclude that it means we should be helpful to others no matter who they are. But such an understanding does not take into account the extremes of pain and suffering that Christians experience for saying "No" to the wicked. How do you do good to someone who has done evil to you? Paul is not just writing about a person who gives you a dirty look or says something painful. He is thinking of the Thessalonians living under the threat of persecution for the faith. They must somehow do good and return kindness when severely mistreated. The word translated "seek" has the sense of "pursue" or "chase" and was used to describe persecution. Paul turned the term around to describe how a Christian who is hunted down by the persecutor must hunt for a way to do good for that persecutor. The expression accents the challenge of figuring out what is truly good and right to do for someone so offensive. How one responds will vary, depending on the circumstances. But one thing will not change: Christians are challenged to forgive those who wrong them and to have mercy upon them.

5:12–15 in Devotion and Prayer. We should respect the pastors of our congregations because of their work for the Lord and the whole people of God. Although the Lord of the Church provides these leaders to labor among us and to be over us in the Lord, all Christians have an obligation to speak the Word of God to others. The Lord also calls us to pursue the good of others, including those outside the Church and those who would persecute the Church. • "Give us lips to sing Thy glory, Tongues Thy mercy to proclaim, Throats that shout the hope that fills us, Mouths to speak Thy holy name. Alleluia, alleluia! May the light which Thou dost send Fill our songs with alleluias, Alleluias without end!" Amen. (*LSB* 578:5).

The evaluation of prophecy (5:16–22)

ESV	KJV
¹⁶Rejoice always, ¹⁷pray without ceasing, ¹⁸give thanks in all circumstances; for this is the will of God in Christ Jesus for you. ¹⁹Do not quench the Spirit. ²⁰Do not despise prophecies, ²¹but test everything; hold fast what is good. ²²Abstain from every form of evil.	¹⁶Rejoice evermore. ¹⁷Pray without ceasing. ¹⁸In every thing give thanks: for this is the will of God in Christ Jesus concerning you. ¹⁹Quench not the Spirit. ²⁰Despise not prophesyings. ²¹Prove all things; hold fast that which is good. ²²Abstain from all appearance of evil.

Introduction to 5:16–22 Paul then shared shorter, general instructions for believers. Yet his teaching here is still given with a view to the priority of the Word of God in the life of the congregation. These verses at the center of the section from vv. 12–28 follow after the apostle's extensive teaching on the end times (4:13–5:11). In view of this, they provide a special sense of urgency. For Paul was speaking of things that are especially important for being ready when Christ returns in glory.

5:16–18 Joy, prayer, and thanksgiving form a unity. Even though God has other purposes for us, this triad is certainly His will for us as expressed in personal or family prayer and in congregational devotion.

5:16 Paul did not mean by this short statement that Christians should go about with plastic smiles, pretending that everything is great and wonderful when in fact it is not. Christian joy is not so shallow but, if it is to be constant, must well up from something much deeper than ourselves, our emotions, and our circumstances. Paul pointed the Thessalonians to the hope that is in the Lord. Elsewhere he explained that joy is a fruit of the Spirit (Gal 5:22–23) and the natural overflow of faith that trusts in so great and caring a Lord.

5:17 We cannot verbally pray at all times, but it is possible to be in the spirit of prayer and ever ready to pray (see also 1:2 and note). Luther wrote, "The Lord's Prayer has also been prescribed so that we should see and consider the distress that ought to drive and compel us to pray without ceasing" (LC III 24). Other reformers described the ready attitude of prayer as follows, "We should ask that through the same Spirit and His grace, by means of the daily exercise of reading and doing God's Word, He would preserve in us faith and His heavenly gifts, strengthen us from day to day, and keep us to the end" (FC SD II 16).

5:18 *will of God in Christ.* Paul earlier told the Thessalonians that sanctification is God's will for them (4:3). Here, it finds expression in their joy, prayer, and thanksgiving. Sanctification is about more than avoiding bad behavior. A person made whole in Christ actively seeks God's will and takes joy in Him. Wesley wrote,

> Prayer may be said to be the breath of our spiritual life. He that lives cannot possibly cease breathing. So much as we really enjoy of the presence of God, so much prayer and praise do we offer up without ceasing; else our rejoicing is but delusion. Thanksgiving is inseparable from true prayer. It is almost essentially connected with it. He that always prays, is ever giving praise, whether in ease or pain; both for prosperity and for the greatest adversity. (Wesley 531).

5:19 Fire symbolized the Holy Spirit (cf. Ac 2:3–4); hence, "quenching" the Holy Spirit would involve activity that would undermine the Spirit's Word. Some connect this phrase with "prophecies" in v. 20, as if Paul had advised the Thessalonians not to put out the spiritual gifts working among them. However, the scope of this imperative is more general and includes any behavior that would grieve the Holy Spirit, such as idleness, immorality, or false teaching. The Spirit would set every aspect of the believer's life aglow with the light of the Gospel.

5:20 Some Thessalonians might have valued the spectacular gifts (e.g., tongues) more than prophecy. In writing to the Corinthians, Paul noted that "prophecy" (speaking the Word of God in its truth and purity) is the foremost gift of the Spirit (1Co 14:1–2). Prophets in both the OT and NT exhorted and spoke God's will for their specific situation and for the future. In biblical language, "prophecy" refers not only to predicting the future (foretelling) but also to all faithful speaking of God's Word (forthtelling).

5:21 *test.* The Thessalonians (and all Christians) could "test" all things by determining if they were consistent with the Word of God (cf. Rm 12:2). Related to this would be testing the prophet's testimony to Christ—does he accept the lordship of Christ (1Co 12:3)? Paul even encouraged Christians to test themselves to see whether they were in the faith (2Co 13:5). To be of God, teaching must agree with what God has revealed to us in His Word (see Dt 18:20; 1Co 14:29–38; 2Co 13:5; 1Jn 4:1). The Lutheran reformers concluded, "The Holy Scriptures alone remain the judge, rule, and norm. According to them—as the only touchstone—all teachings shall and must be discerned and judged" (FC Ep Sum 7).

5:22 *evil.* Paul turned from warning against false prophetic utterances (v. 21) to warning against every kind of evil. See the note at 4:3. Evil certainly comes in different forms. It may be either blatant or subtle, from without the Church or from within. Therefore, the Lord equips us with the breastplate of faith and love and with the helmet of hope (5:8).

5:16–22 in Devotion and Prayer Paul speaks to those living in the knowledge that they could expect the return of Christ at any time (see the note at 2Th 2:2). His instruction here, therefore, is highly relevant for Christians in any and every era. In pithy statements, he expresses the urgency with which we live. • Lord, give us Your heart and mind so that our lives may be blameless, respecting and loving others. In Jesus' name we pray. Amen.

PART 3

CONCLUSION (5:23–28)

ESV	KJV
[23]Now may the God of peace himself sanctify you completely, and may your whole spirit and soul and body be kept blameless at the coming of our Lord Jesus Christ. [24]He who calls you is faithful; he will surely do it. [25]Brothers, pray for us. [26]Greet all the brothers with a holy kiss. [27]I put you under oath before the Lord to have this letter read to all the brothers. [28]The grace of our Lord Jesus Christ be with you.	[23]And the very God of peace sanctify you wholly; and I pray God your whole spirit and soul and body be preserved blameless unto the coming of our Lord Jesus Christ. [24]Faithful is he that calleth you, who also will do it. [25]Brethren, pray for us. [26]Greet all the brethren with an holy kiss. [27]I charge you by the Lord that this epistle be read unto all the holy brethren. [28]The grace of our Lord Jesus Christ be with you. Amen.

Introduction to 5:23–28 Paul tersely concluded this Letter with both blessings and instructions. This conclusion emphasized the corporate life of the Thessalonian congregation.

5:23 *sanctify you completely.* Sanctification is the practical result of God's peace-giving work in our life through the Holy Spirit. God's sanctification of us through faith in His Son, Jesus Christ, extends to our whole person—we are sanctified thoroughly. Complete sanctification will be ours in eternity. See further the note at 4:3. *spirit and soul and body.* The entire person, outside and inside, should be sanctified. These three terms denote three different ways of looking at the physical and non-physical aspects of human nature. They are not intended to be a complete list of component parts, which, when added together, make up a human being. Philosophers have argued about whether a human being has two parts (dichotomy) or three

131

parts (trichotomy). Some will refer to this passage to defend the idea that there are three parts. But such debates are misplaced and should be abandoned. For example, in Mk 12:30 Jesus quoted an OT passage that lists four aspects of a human being. Should one then argue that a person is "quadro-chotomous"? That would be silly (and difficult to say, too). These are just descriptive lists that might be expanded or shortened. *blameless at the coming of our Lord Jesus Christ.* See the note at 3:13. The second coming of our Lord will bring our Christian journey here on earth to its conclusion. Those who are sanctified by faith in the Lord will be like the wise virgins who had their oil lamps ready when the bridegroom came (Mt 25:1–13). Cf. 1Th 4:13–18.

5:24 God has called us and is calling us through His Word. The initiative is from Him. From God's calling in His Gospel, we can know that He has elected us unto salvation. See Jn 6:44 and the notes at 2Th 2:13–14. *will surely do it.* Compare what the apostle wrote in Php 1:6.

5:25 Paul revealed humility by requesting the intercession of others on his behalf. It is a natural part of the Christian life to desire and request the prayers of others.

5:26 *holy kiss.* This was a common way in that culture of sharing the peace of the Lord; this may have even been a liturgical term and practice. See also Rm 16:16; 1Co 16:20; 2Co 13:12. Opinions differ about whether this was a literal kiss somewhere on the face or whether it was touching cheek-to-cheek with a kissing sound like greetings between familiar persons that still prevail in some European countries. It is possible that these European greetings are actually cultural remnants of the Christian "holy kiss." However, some commentators believe the holy kiss was an embrace rather than a kiss with the mouth.

5:27 *oath.* Paul was asking the Thessalonians to promise that they would read the Letter in front of the whole congregation. There is a strong biblical basis for taking oaths or vows. For example, in Nu 30 Moses dedicated an entire chapter to the topic. However, some Christian interpreters point to Jesus' words in Mt 5:34 and conclude that Christians should never take an oath, an idea that results in a contradiction with what Paul taught here. When you read Mt 5:34, note that Jesus rejected swearing "by" something as a way of intensifying one's oath. Jesus was not speaking against taking oaths but our attempts to make our words stronger by adding something else.

In other words, Jesus commanded Christians to simply do what they promise, which fits nicely with Paul's request to the Thessalonians. *letter read to all the brothers.* Paul knew that communication, particularly that of the Gospel, was central for people to be saved and to be formed in Christ (Rm 10:14). Therefore, he emphasized that the written word be heard by all. This injunction by the apostle, like the similar one in his Letter to the Colossians, is an indication that his Letters are to be regarded as the Word of God, on a par with the OT Scriptures. See the note at Col 4:16. One may see in Paul's admonition the beginning of the NT Scriptures as an authority in the lives of God's people.

5:28 Instead of using the customary secular ending for "farewell," Paul closed his Letter with a grace benediction—just as he had started it (1:1). The apostle gave grace "the last word" as well as the first, indicating the central importance of the undeserved favor of God in our salvation (see similar use of "grace" at Col 1:2; 4:18).

5:23–28 in Devotion and Prayer The life of God's people together is to be focused around the Word of God, fellowship, and prayer (cf. Ac 2:42). He calls us to keep our promises even as He keeps His promise of grace to us in our only Savior, Jesus Christ.
• "Holy Spirit, ever working Through the Church's ministry; Quick'ning, strength'ning, and absolving, Setting captive sinners free; Holy Spirit, ever binding Age to age and soul to soul In communion never ending, You we worship and extol." Amen. (*LSB* 650:3; *H82* 511:2)

2 THESSALONIANS

INTRODUCTION TO
2 THESSALONIANS

Overview

Author

Paul the apostle

Date

c. AD 52

Place

Thessalonica

People

Paul; Silvanus; Timothy; Thessalonian Church; persecutors

Purpose

To correct misunderstandings about Christ's return that had arisen after

Paul and his co-workers left Thessalonica

Law and Sin Themes

Steadfastness; affliction; eternal destruction; man of lawlessness; idleness

Grace and Gospel Themes

The Gospel message; God's righteousness; Jesus gathers us; the Spirit sanctifies us

Memory Verses

Grow in faith and increase in love (1:3); stand firm (2:15)

Luther on 2 Thessalonians

In the first epistle [5:2], Paul had resolved for the Thessalonians the question of the Last Day, telling them that it would come quickly, as a thief in the night. Now as is likely to happen—that one question always gives rise to another, because of misunderstanding—the Thessalonians understood that the Last Day was already at hand. Thereupon Paul writes this epistle and explains himself.

In chapter 1 he comforts them with the eternal reward of their faith and of their patience amid sufferings of every kind and with the punishment of their persecutors in eternal pain.

In chapter 2 he teaches that before the Last Day, the Roman Empire must first pass away, and Antichrist set himself up as God in Christendom and seduce the unbelieving world with false doctrines and signs—until Christ shall come and destroy him by his glorious coming, first slaying him with spiritual preaching.

In chapter 3 he gives some admonitions, especially that they rebuke the idlers who are not supporting themselves by their own labor. If the idlers will not reform, then the faithful shall avoid them. And this is a stiff rebuke to the clergy of our day. (LW 35:387–88)

Calvin on 2 Thessalonians

It does not appear to me probable that this Epistle was sent from Rome, as the Greek manuscripts commonly bear; for he would have made some mention of his bonds, as he is accustomed to do in other Epistles. . . . The occasion, however, of his writing was this—that the Thessalonians might not reckon themselves overlooked, because Paul had not visited them, when hastening to another quarter. (Calvin 309)

Gerhard on 2 Thessalonians

The occasion for the writing of 2 Thessalonians was this: Some of the Thessalonians were understanding what the apostle had written in c[hapters]. 3–4 of the first Epistle regarding the immediate coming of Christ as if the Day of the Lord were already upon them. In this Epistle, the apostle wanted to resist this false opinion. (Gerhard E 1.265)

Challenges for Readers

Paul's Authorship. Some scholars have questioned the authenticity of this Letter, specifically regarding Paul's authorship, chiefly due to seeming differences between 1 Thessalonians and 2 Thessalonians regarding the return of Christ. Paul mentioned issues of forgery (2:2; 3:17), but this hardly suggests that the Letter itself is forged. In 2 Thessalonians, Paul taught that the day of the Lord had not yet come, which accords well with 1Th 5:2. In the second Letter, Paul sought to calm the readers about the imminence of Christ's return (2:2), which is simply a difference in emphasis from 1 Thessalonians, not doctrine. The two Epistles are simply emphasizing different but complementary aspects of the teaching on the end times: that we cannot know the time of our Lord's return, and yet there will be signs. Bishop Polycarp affirmed the Pauline authorship of 2 Thessalonians and its divinely authoritative status around AD 110. We can in good conscience agree with his conclusion.

Man of Lawlessness. Paul makes special reference to apostasy and the exaltation of the "lawless one" (2:3–10), which must take place before Christ's return in judgment. Though his descriptions of these events are unique, the same themes are taught in other parts of Scripture. According to the Early Church father Irenaeus (*ANF* 1:535–56), the lawless one corresponds to the "spirit of the antichrist" (1Jn 2:18; 4:3) and the beast (and/or the prostitute "Babylon"; Rv 13:1–10; chs. 17–18).

The Restrainer. Paul makes a passing reference to someone or something that restrains the appearance of the "man of lawlessness" (2:7). The Church Fathers commonly referred to God restraining the lawless one through Roman governance, but other suggestions have been offered (e.g., the Gospel, the Holy Spirit—suggestions that do not fit well with Paul's broader theology). In any case, note that the restraint comes from God, no matter what the means may be. Cf. Dn 10:13, 21; Rv 12:7; 20:1–3.

Blessings for Readers

As in 1 Thessalonians, Paul exhibits exemplary pastoral care for the Thessalonian congregation. He patiently explains issues of doctrine that have confused them and instructs them consistently in matters of faith and life, according to the traditions that he had taught them (2:15). The second Letter to the Thessalonians is an outstanding example of the spiritual tact of the apostle, which enables him to quell the fevered excitement of a hope grown hysterical without quenching the fervor and the life-shaping force of that hope, and to instill sobriety without robbing the Christian hope of its intensity, leaving both fear and faith to do their salutary work in man. The apostle's emphasis on work (an emphasis that he spelled out in his life too, by supporting himself) recognizes the order that God the Creator established. It remains one of the great safeguards of Christian sanity over against all falsely spiritual contempt for earthly concerns.

The second chapter renews and explicates the warning of Jesus, who taught His disciples that wheat and weeds must ripen together till the harvest; it reminds the Church that the satanic counterthrust is inevitable and constant wherever God's Word grows and God's reign is established. Any shallow optimism that bows the knee to the idol of progress and any churchly piety that becomes comfortably at home with worldly standards of right and wrong is a denial of the revelation on which the life of the Church is built.

Outline

  I. The Greeting (1:1–2)

 II. The Thanksgiving (1:3–12)
     A. Thanks for Faith and Love (1:3–4)
     B. Encouragement of the Discouraged (1:5–10)
     C. Petition for Worthy Conduct (1:11–12)

III. Exhortation and Encouragement about the End Times (ch. 2)
     A. Events Preceding the Coming of the Day of the Lord (2:1–12)
     B. Encouragement and Thanksgiving (2:13–17)

IV. Apostolic Commands (3:1–15)
     A. Request for Prayers (3:1–5)
     B. Discipline of the Disorderly (3:6–12)
     C. Admonition to Do Good (3:13–15)

 V. Conclusion (3:16–18)
     A. Prayer for Peace (3:16)
     B. Greeting (3:17)
     C. Benediction (3:18)

PART 1

GREETING AND THANKSGIVING (CH. 1)

Thessalonians (1:2–10)

ESV	KJV
1 ¹Paul, Silvanus, and Timothy, To the church of the Thessalonians in God our Father and the Lord Jesus Christ: ²Grace to you and peace from God our Father and the Lord Jesus Christ.	1 ¹Paul, and Silvanus, and Timotheus, unto the church of the Thessalonians in God our Father and the Lord Jesus Christ: ²Grace unto you, and peace, from God our Father and the Lord Jesus Christ.

Introduction to 1:1–2 Paul began his second Letter to the Thessalonians in almost exactly the same words as he used in the greeting for the first Letter. He included the same brethren as co-authors. Yet Paul twice used the word "our" in addressing his readers (see note below). See the introduction to Col 1:1–2 on how Paul adapted Greek style to begin his Letters.

1:1 *Silvanus, and Timothy.* See the note at 1Th 1:1. *church.* The Greek term is *ekklesia*, from which we get words such as "ecclesiastical." In the NT it can denote a local Christian congregation (as here) or the Church at large (Eph 1:22). In secular Greek the word referred to any public assembly (Ac 19:32); in the Greek translation of the OT it was used to render Hebrew words referring to Israel as God's chosen people. This dual background to *ekklesia* made it well suited to describe the community of the followers of Jesus Christ: it was the continuation of Israel as the people of God, and it was an assembly open to anyone who embraced Jesus as Savior and Lord through faith in Him. *Thessalonians.* See the note at 1Th 1:1. *in God.* See the note at 1Th 1:1. *our.* Paul emphasized the bond that God the Father had created between him, his colleagues, and this new congregation at Thessalonica, which included both Jews and Gentiles.

1:2 This is Paul's typical greeting in his Letters. Since the apostle intended for his Letters to be read within the context of worship (see the notes at 1Th 5:27 and Col 4:16), this greeting became a common one within worship (it is still often used in that way today). God's grace is the source of all real blessings, and peace is the result of these blessings. See further 2:16; 3:16.

1:1–2 in Devotion and Prayer Paul greeted the Christians in Thessalonica as fellow members of the Body of Christ (the Church) and blessed them with God's grace and peace. Christian believers are called out of worldliness to lives of holiness. We are connected to the heavenly Father, to the Creator Himself. As such, we must act differently than the sinful world and not according to its standards of self-centeredness (cf. Rm 12:1–2); God calls us to exhibit grace and peace to all others. Like the Thessalonians, our place as Christians "in God our Father and the Lord Jesus Christ" is a new creation gift from God and is assured to us by His grace alone (cf. Eph 1:11–14). Jesus' death and resurrection incorporated us into His Body through Baptism and reconciled us with the Father (cf. Gal 2:20; Eph 2:13–21).

• "Lord Jesus Christ, Your pow'r make known, For You are Lord of lords alone; Defend Your holy Church that we May sing Your praise eternally. O Comforter of priceless worth, Send peace and unity on earth; Support us in our final strife And lead us out of death to life." Amen. (*LSB* 655:2–3)

Thanks for Faith and Love (1:3–4)

ESV	KJV
[3]We ought always to give thanks to God for you, brothers, as is right, because your faith is growing abundantly, and the love of every one of you for one another is increasing. [4]Therefore we ourselves boast about you in the churches of God for your steadfastness and faith in all your persecutions and in the afflictions that you are enduring.	[3]We are bound to thank God always for you, brethren, as it is meet, because that your faith groweth exceedingly, and the charity of every one of you all toward each other aboundeth; [4]So that we ourselves glory in you in the churches of God for your patience and faith in all your persecutions and tribulations that ye endure:

Introduction to 1:3–4 After the greeting of his Letters, Paul customarily continued with a section of thanksgiving (this was a common feature of all letter writing in that time and place). The present Letter is noteworthy in that the apostle gave thanks for how the Thessalonians had met persecution with a growing faith. To his thanksgiving Paul added boasting before the Church and the world. The Thessalonians showed themselves to be exceptional brethren.

1:3 *give thanks.* Calvin wrote,

> In these words Paul shews that we are bound to give thanks to God, not only when he does us good, but also when we take into view the favours bestowed by him upon our brethren. For wherever the goodness of God shines forth, it becomes us to extol it. Farther, the welfare of our brethren ought to be so dear to us, that we ought to reckon among our own benefits everything that has been conferred upon them. Nay more, if we consider the nature and sacredness of the unity of Christ's body, such a mutual fellowship will have place among us, that we shall reckon the benefits conferred upon an individual member as gain to the whole Church. Hence, in extolling God's benefits, we must always have an eye to the whole body of the Church. (Calvin 312)

faith is growing abundantly . . . love . . . is increasing. The Greek word translated "growing abundantly" describes growth that reaches its further extent, such as a mature, fruit bearing plant. The apostle had labored in the Word and prayer, so that these very things might take place in the Thessalonians (cf. 1Th 3:10, 12). Jesus often chided His disciples for having little faith or weak faith, which needed to grow. Faith is a gift from God, created through His means of grace (cf. Lk 17:5 where the disciples' request refers to God's giving them faith; Eph 2:8). Through these means, God also grows our faith. He matures and strengthens our confidence and trust in Jesus as our only Savior (cf. Mk 9:24). Melanchthon shared Paul's emphasis on faith and wrote, "We must use the Sacraments in such a way that faith, which believes the promises offered and set forth through the Sacraments, is increased" (AC XIII 2). Faith is not completed or made better by love; faith is sufficient in and of itself to connect us with God's salvation. However, faith grows in understanding, becomes steadier in the face of persecution, and naturally produces good works (love) for the neighbor who needs them. Through faith, a person has been made a new creation, a good tree that produces more and more good fruit. Love increases as faith grows (cf. Mt 7:17, 12:33–35; 2Co 5:17; LC II 57–59; III 1–3).

1:4 *boast.* While forms of this word can refer to the sin of boasting (Rm 1:30; 3:27), here it plainly has a positive meaning. Paul and his coworkers were glad to speak of the Thessalonians as an example of faith and love for other churches to emulate (cf. 2Co 8:1–7). *churches of God.* This would refer particularly to churches in Corinth and its surrounding area, from where Paul was writing (cf. 2Co 1:1). *persecutions.* Specifics of the Thessalonians' suffering (beyond what is recorded in Ac 17:1–9, 13) are not revealed, except that it is for "the kingdom of God" (v. 5). Christian suffering is in many ways a mystery of the faith. Why should the upright and honest people of Thessalonica have to suffer? Yet Paul gave thanks! After all, a Christian will and must suffer (2Tm 3:12). Furthermore, persecution is a sign that a person is on the right way: the powers of evil are disturbed when Christ is active and when His promised coming is near. For example, suffering mysteriously unifies us with Jesus, the Suffering Servant (cf. Is 53). It provides an opportunity for us to give glory to God (cf. Jn 9:1–3). It tests and strengthens our faith (cf. 1Pt 1:3–9). It teaches us to love God for His own sake, and not for the sake of prosperity. It conforms and shapes us into the image of Christ (cf. Rm 8:17). It teaches us to glory in the cross (cf. Lk 9:22–24; Ps 34:19–22). It humbles us, reminding us that the servant is not greater than the master and preventing self-righteousness from closing us to His gifts (cf. Jn 15:20). No wonder the Thessalonians were growing despite their suffering! Suffering can be thought of as one of God's "strange" gifts (cf. Ac 5:40–42; 1Pt 4:12–14) that actually works for our benefit or the benefit of others around us. See further the note on suffering and affliction at Col 1:24.

1:3–4 in Devotion and Prayer Paul gave thanks for God's grace at work among the Thessalonians, by which He had created faith and love in them. Paul pointed to the persecuted Thessalonians as examples for other Christians of their time and for all subsequent eras of history. We, too, should "be imitators of God" (Eph 5:1). He calls us to set an example to others in what we believe and in what we say and do for them; i.e., by living in faith and in love. In this way, we will be, as Luther puts it, little Christs, "[helping] our neighbor through our body and its works" (LW 31:367). Christ is indeed our example, but, much greater and higher than that, He is our Savior! Cf.

1Pt 2:19–25. He suffered in our place, on account of our sins, for us!
• "When life's troubles rise to meet me, Though their weight May be great, They will not defeat me. God, my loving Savior, sends them; He who knows All my woes Knows how best to end them." Amen. (*LSB* 756:2)

Encouragement of the Discouraged (1:5–10)

ESV	KJV
⁵This is evidence of the righteous judgment of God, that you may be considered worthy of the kingdom of God, for which you are also suffering—⁶since indeed God considers it just to repay with affliction those who afflict you, ⁷and to grant relief to you who are afflicted as well as to us, when the Lord Jesus is revealed from heaven with his mighty angels ⁸in flaming fire, inflicting vengeance on those who do not know God and on those who do not obey the gospel of our Lord Jesus. ⁹They will suffer the punishment of eternal destruction, away from the presence of the Lord and from the glory of his might, ¹⁰when he comes on that day to be glorified in his saints, and to be marveled at among all who have believed, because our testimony to you was believed.	⁵Which is a manifest token of the righteous judgment of God, that ye may be counted worthy of the kingdom of God, for which ye also suffer: ⁶Seeing it is a righteous thing with God to recompense tribulation to them that trouble you; ⁷And to you who are troubled rest with us, when the Lord Jesus shall be revealed from heaven with his mighty angels, ⁸In flaming fire taking vengeance on them that know not God, and that obey not the gospel of our Lord Jesus Christ: ⁹Who shall be punished with everlasting destruction from the presence of the Lord, and from the glory of his power; ¹⁰When he shall come to be glorified in his saints, and to be admired in all them that believe (because our testimony among you was believed) in that day.

Introduction to 1:5–12 As with 1Th, teaching on the end times plays a major role in the message of 2Th. They were greatly interested in the reappearing of Jesus but had some questions and anxieties about it. Here the apostle presented the second coming and the life to come as both comfort for God's people and judgment on the unbelieving. The reappearing of Christ Jesus will, in turn, serve as a vindication for the faith that the believers put in Christ, even in the face of their suffering for that faith.

1:5 Paul consoled the Thessalonians. As the Last Day drew nearer, their suffering, as well as their faith and conduct in the face of tribulation, was part of God's plan of history. Moreover, their life under persecution was a clear sign of the Almighty's future "righteous judgment." Faith preserved them unto eternal life (cf. 1Pt 1:3–7). *This is evidence.* Likely refers to "your steadfastness and faith in all your persecutions" (v. 4), which illustrates the genuineness of their faith. *worthy of the kingdom of God.* On "the kingdom of God," see the note at Col 1:13. Paul taught significantly less than Jesus did on the topic of "kingdom." His preferred terms were increasingly "church" and "heaven," which become synonyms for Jesus' teaching about the earthly and eternal reign of God. Paul also taught that suffering is at times an aspect of the Father's gracious discipline; it is a way in which He shapes and conforms His children, thus preparing them for the glory of His kingdom. God Himself makes us worthy through Jesus, the Lamb (cf. v. 11; Gal 3:27; Rv 5:6–14).

1:6 *repay with affliction.* This is a description of what will take place at the second coming of Christ (cf. vv. 7–10). God's justice will be appropriate toward the wicked, in accordance with their rebellion and wickedness. Just as those who are righteous by faith will be rewarded for the fruit of their faith (1Co 3:11–15), so those whose unbelief bears the fruit of unrighteousness will be repaid proportionately (Rv 22:12).

1:7 *mighty angels.* This may be an indication that the Lord will execute His powerful judgment through His angels (cf. Ps 103:20). On the other hand, this passage may intend to assert simply that the angels will accompany Christ when He comes again in glory (Mt 25:31). See note, 1Th 3:13.

1:8 *in flaming fire.* Fire accompanies and reveals the Lord as He comes "to judge the living and the dead" (1Pt 4:5) in vengeance (cf. Dn 7:9–10). Fire is also associated with the majestic presence of God (e.g., Ex 3:2; Rv 1:13–14). *know God.* In a passage like this, "knowing" God means more than mere intellectual knowledge about Him; it refers to being in a relationship (cf. Gn 4:1) with Him, in this case, being in a favorable relationship with Him through faith in Christ (cf. Eph 4:13; Ti 1:1). *obey the gospel.* Expressions such as "obey the gospel" occur regularly in the Scriptures as a description of saving faith. However, there may be a danger of misunderstanding this way of speaking, as though faith were a good work by which we please God. Since the Greek word for obey/obedience is a compound of the word for hear/listen, perhaps it is helpful to think of faith as listening to and heeding the Gospel message (as opposed to merely ignoring what is said). Rejection of the Gospel is disobedience to the divine invitation to faith and life. On saving faith, see further the note at 1:3.

1:9 *eternal destruction, away from the presence.* Everlasting fire, chastisement, ruin, punishment, and judgment describe the end of the wicked who do not heed God's mercy and warnings. Thus, death as the opposite of "eternal life" (e.g., Rm 6:23) is not an annihilation but a complete and final separation from God, from beholding the face of Jesus, and therefore separation from all that is good and abandonment to all that is loathsome. Wesley wrote,

> As there can be no end of their sins, (the same enmity against God continuing,) so neither of their punishment: sin and its punishment running parallel throughout eternity itself. They must of necessity therefore be cut off from all good and all possibility of it. (Wesley 534)

Eternal separation from the presence of God is what makes hell the horror that it is; this separation from God's presence gives us insight into the sadness in the words of Jesus from the cross, "My God, My God, why have You forsaken Me?" (Mt 27:46; Mk 15:34). We may rightly think of hell as a prison that holds the wicked away from those righteous by God's grace. God did not create hell because He delights in punishment but because He delights to save His people from those who would ruin them. Cf. Mt 25:41. *glory of His might.* This refers to the visible glory of God's presence. It shines forth from His strength, His might. Our Lord's presence is held in tension: earthly in this time and place, and also heavenly in eternity. He is inseparably present with the faithful already now in His Body, the Church, through Word and Sacrament (cf. Rm 8:30–39). At the same time, paradoxically, believers await the revelation of His presence "when He comes on that day" (v. 10). Cf. 2Co 4:6; 1Th 2:12.

1:10 *glorified in His saints.* The Lord ultimately shares His glory with His followers "on that day." He is the source of glory (cf. 2:14; Rm 8:17–18; Php 3:21). In the present passage the phrase may instead be a synonym for "marveled at among all who have believed," which describes the awe with which believers worshiped God. Consider, for example, the common expression, "Give glory to God." The expression invites the question, "How? What glory could a sinner possible give to God?" Of course we can add nothing to God's glory, but the expression really means that we praise and worship God for the glory He already possesses (Jsh 7:19; Is 42:12). *saints.* The saints are those who are holy before God through faith in Christ. See further the notes at Col 1:2; 1Th 4:3. *testimony.* This term refers to the Gospel (v. 8) preached by the apostles, who were witnesses of what they had seen and heard, especially the utterly convincing fact that Jesus was raised from the dead (1Co 15:5–8).

Petition for Worthy Conduct (1:11–12)

ESV	KJV
[11]To this end we always pray for you, that our God may make you worthy of his calling and may fulfill every resolve for good and every work of faith by his power, [12]so that the name of our Lord Jesus may be glorified in you, and you in him, according to the grace of our God and the Lord Jesus Christ.	[11]Wherefore also we pray always for you, that our God would count you worthy of this calling, and fulfil all the good pleasure of his goodness, and the work of faith with power: [12]That the name of our Lord Jesus Christ may be glorified in you, and ye in him, according to the grace of our God and the Lord Jesus Christ.

1:11 *worthy of His calling.* See the note at v. 5. Only God can proclaim and make the Thessalonians or anyone worthy, and "He will surely do it" (1Th 5:24)! Here the worthiness before God is what we received as a result of our forgiveness through faith in Christ. *calling.* In this case, the calling to faith and salvation is in view. (Especially in other passages [e.g., 1Co 7:17–24], "calling" may also refer to our present vocations and our holiness therein.) God calls Christians in Baptism, and thus He saves them, draws them to Himself, and keeps them in His hand. *every resolve for good and every work of faith.* God's gift of justifying faith produces these good works. These are wrought by God's sanctifying power. Though justification and sanctification are distinct, as are faith and works, they are never separate. We are saved through faith alone, but faith is never alone; it always produces good works. *by His power.* Because of sin, we are powerless to do the good works of faith. The Lord Himself provides us the power to do good works (cf. Eph 2:10) that truly please Him and bless our neighbors. Paul's prayer is that God would continue His work and bring it to completion (cf. Jn 15:5). See also the note at v. 3.

1:12 *so that the name of our Lord Jesus may be glorified.* In and through His people, the Lord is glorified and He, in turn, is their glory. Luther wrote, "[God] has created us for this very reason, that He might redeem and sanctify us" (LC II 64). The Westminster Shorter Catechism states, "Man's chief end is to glorify God, and to enjoy him forever" (Schaff III:676). Christians glorify the Lord by serving their neighbor (cf. Mt 25:40; Lk 10:25–37; Rm 12:1). Bengel wrote, "We confer nothing on the Lord, whereas the Lord really confers upon us salvation; and hence His name is glorified in us; and we ourselves moreover in Him" (Bengel 216). Our good service to others is the highest praise we can offer to the Lord. This service has an evangelistic effect (Mt 5:16; cf. Php 1:9–11) as people learn about God's love and mercy through the love and mercy we extend to them in His name. Although Christians dare not confine themselves to being "silent witnesses," they also must not fail to proclaim the Gospel without accompanying kindness, lest the Gospel sound strange coming from lips of lazy, self-interested saints. *grace.* See the note at Col 1:6. *our God and the Lord.* Paul normally used "God" to refer to the First Person of the Holy Trinity (the Father) and "Lord" to refer to the Second Person (the Son). Both persons are divine; Paul was speaking here of the first two persons of the Trinity, not two separate gods.

1:5–12 in Devotion and Prayer The Lord Jesus will carry out God's judgment at His second coming on the Last Day. This is bad news for those who do not believe, for those who reject God's grace in Christ (v. 8), as "they will suffer . . . away from the presence of the Lord" (v. 9). As believers, we live in a state of continual readiness for this day (cf. Mt 24:36–51; 2Co 6:2). Jesus will be glorified in us, and we in Him (v. 12); by His grace, God will judge believers worthy to inherit heaven; and by His power, He will bring our faith to its heavenly fulfillment (vv. 11–12). • "The clouds of judgment gather, The time is growing late; Be sober and be watchful, Our judge is at the gate: The judge who comes in mercy, The judge who comes in might To put an end to evil And diadem the right." Amen. (*LSB* 513:1)

PART 2

EXHORTATION AND ENCOURAGEMENT ABOUT THE END TIMES (CH. 2)

Events Preceding the Coming of the Day of the Lord (2:1–12)

ESV	KJV
2 ¹Now concerning the coming of our Lord Jesus Christ and our being gathered together to him, we ask you, brothers, ²not to be quickly shaken in mind or alarmed, either by a spirit or a spoken word, or a letter seeming to be from us, to the effect that the day of the Lord has come. ³Let no one deceive you in any way. For that day will not come, unless the rebellion comes first, and the man of lawlessness is revealed, the son of destruction, ⁴who opposes and exalts himself against every so-called god or object of worship, so that he takes his seat in the temple of God, proclaiming himself to be God. ⁵Do you not remember that when I was still with you I told you these things? ⁶And you know what is restraining him now so that he may be revealed in his time. ⁷For the mystery of lawlessness is already at work. Only he who now restrains it will do so until he is out of the way.	2 ¹Now we beseech you, brethren, by the coming of our Lord Jesus Christ, and by our gathering together unto him, ²That ye be not soon shaken in mind, or be troubled, neither by spirit, nor by word, nor by letter as from us, as that the day of Christ is at hand. ³Let no man deceive you by any means: for that day shall not come, except there come a falling away first, and that man of sin be revealed, the son of perdition; ⁴Who opposeth and exalteth himself above all that is called God, or that is worshipped; so that he as God sitteth in the temple of God, shewing himself that he is God. ⁵Remember ye not, that, when I was yet with you, I told you these things? ⁶And now ye know what withholdeth that he might be revealed in his time. ⁷For the mystery of iniquity doth already work: only he who now letteth will let, until he be taken out of the way.

⁸And then the lawless one will be revealed, whom the Lord Jesus will kill with the breath of his mouth and bring to nothing by the appearance of his coming. ⁹The coming of the lawless one is by the activity of Satan with all power and false signs and wonders, ¹⁰and with all wicked deception for those who are perishing, because they refused to love the truth and so be saved. ¹¹Therefore God sends them a strong delusion, so that they may believe what is false, ¹²in order that all may be condemned who did not believe the truth but had pleasure in unrighteousness.	⁸And then shall that Wicked be revealed, whom the Lord shall consume with the spirit of his mouth, and shall destroy with the brightness of his coming: ⁹Even him, whose coming is after the working of Satan with all power and signs and lying wonders, ¹⁰And with all deceivableness of unrighteousness in them that perish; because they received not the love of the truth, that they might be saved. ¹¹And for this cause God shall send them strong delusion, that they should believe a lie: ¹²That they all might be damned who believed not the truth, but had pleasure in unrighteousness.

Introduction to 2:1–12 In this section Paul offered the Thessalonians teaching about the Last Day, so that they would not be lead astray by false teachings concerning this matter. In these verses he spoke of "the man of lawlessness . . . the son of perdition." It is generally agreed that this passage is one of several biblical texts that speak of what has come to be called "the Antichrist;" other such passages would include Dn 9:24–27; 11:36–45; Mt 24:15 (Mk 13:14); 1Jn 2:18–22; 4:13; 2Jn 7; and Rv 13:1–18.

The history of the interpretation of these passages is a study all to itself, as many different and even contradictory interpretations have been offered. Here is a summary of two common mistaken views: (1) Some claim that this "Antichrist" figure is Satan himself. A close look at the "Antichrist" passages will clearly reveal that while Satan works through "Antichrist," "Antichrist" is distinct from Satan. (2) Others have tried to identify this figure with a single individual. Some, for example, would claim that a particular biblical passage is pointing to Emperor Nero as the Antichrist. Those who suggest such identifications often assume that the biblical author was incorrect about what he wrote. Clearly such an approach is incompatible with a view of Scripture as the inspired Word of God.

A more satisfying approach to "Antichrist" recognizes that there have been many manifestations of "Antichrist" throughout history. Passages such as 2Th 2:1–12 give us a glimpse into the reality of "Antichrist" and how it manifests itself. Although the interpretation of some details remains somewhat mysterious and puzzling, there are enough clear points in the present passage and similar ones to enable us to grasp its overall meaning.

2:1 Paul began by referring back to his earlier teaching. He had taught the Thessalonians about these matters when he was with them, but their continuing questions made it necessary for him to write his first Letter to them (1Th). In this Letter he would clarify matters more, in so far as he was able to explain these mysteries. *coming.* See the note at 1Th 4:15. *our being gathered together in Him.* See the note at 1Th 4:17.

2:2 *not to be quickly shaken.* Evidently the apostle had received word that the Thessalonians were greatly troubled by the (mistaken) report that they had missed out on Christ's coming and its blessings. Consider times when you have missed an important phone call or when you were supposed to meet someone and found yourself waiting, not knowing whether you were at the right place or whether you somehow missed the person. The awkwardness of such situations seems small when compared to the issue that concerned these new believers at Thessalonica who wondered whether they had missed the coming of the Lord. *by a spirit or a spoken word.* The report that confused the Thessalonians had come supported by the claim that it had been given through a direct revelation from the Holy Spirit (or perhaps through an angel). Paul did not tell us the source of the report but alluded to a possible source in his next comment. *a letter seeming to be from us.* This could refer to a misinterpretation of 1Th that led to doctrinal error. However, it seems more likely that the reference is to a forged letter to the Thessalonians that claimed to be an authentic letter from the apostle and his coworkers (see further the note at 3:17). That such false letters were written during these early years of the Church is evident from the various writings that early Christians rejected, which were attributed to the apostles (known as *pseudepigrapha*, "falsely signed" documents). Famous examples of this kind of literature are The Epistle of Paul to the Laodiceans, The Correspondence between Seneca and Paul, and The Apocalypse of Paul. These examples were written after the time of the apostle and are surely not the letter Paul referred to here, but they allow us to see the kinds of letters that deceivers might write by borrowing the apostle's name and mimicking his other Letters. *the day of the Lord has come.* While NT authors spoke of the time since the completion of the ministry of Christ as "the last days," "the end of the ages," or in similar ways (e.g., Ac 2:17; 1Co 10:11; 1Pt 1:20), that was far different from claiming that the second coming of Christ had already taken place (1Th 3:13; 1Pt 1:6). False teachers may have distorted the words of the apostles in order to manipulate the Thessalonians (for a similar false teaching see 2Tm 2:17–18) as still happens today when some groups sets dates for the reappearing of Christ and make unusual demands of their followers in view of those dates. Paul began to refute such deception in v. 3. The refutation of this error was one of his main purposes in writing 2Th.

2:3 *rebellion.* The Greek term is *apostasia,* which is the root of the English word "apostasy." The term denotes abandonment of the faith. Betrayal, falsehood, hatred, and lawlessness by misled Christians will be marks of this intrachurch rebellion against God and His truth (Mt 24:9–12). *man of lawlessness.* He comes as the completion of the rebellion. Elsewhere in Scripture, this incarnation of evil is called "the antichrist" and "the beast" (see particularly Dn 11:36–45 and Rv 13:1–18). Luther wrote, "[He] not only is a sinner in his own right, but . . . through false doctrine [he] causes others to sin with him" (LW 41:288). *son of destruction.* The man of lawlessness spreads destruction and will ultimately be destroyed himself, i.e., he is headed for destruction. He embodies the great rebellion against God. He is satanic, perhaps even a person who is possessed by Satan. He had not yet fully come at the time Paul wrote 2Th, but the powers that he embodies, the "mystery of lawlessness" (v. 7), were already active. Judas could well have been a type of the man of lawlessness (Jn 13:27; 17:12). Historical figures from biblical times that behaved like the man of lawlessness include Antiochus IV Epiphanes (Dn 11:21–35) who had pigs sacrificed in the temple at Jerusalem and brutally suppressed God's people in the second century BC. The Roman emperors Gaius Caligula (perhaps included in the prophecy of Mt 14:15; Mk 13:14), Nero, and Domitian also introduced various forms of persecution and false worship. For example, the emperor cult at the time of Domitian may well have served as a "model" of the beasts of Rv 13 (particularly the latter one).

2:4 *exalts himself.* The man of lawlessness exalts himself over both true religion (Christianity) and false (man-made) religion. The Early Church father Irenaeus noted, "Antichrist shall be lifted up, not above Him, but above those which are indeed called gods, but are not" (*ANF* 1:420). The exaltation of the man of lawlessness is part of his deception. *temple of God.* Paul could be using the Jerusalem temple as a symbol of God's authority or rule. (The temple itself was destroyed in AD 70 and so would not be standing at the end of the age.) Cf. Dn 9–12. *proclaiming himself to be God.* This is the height of what could be called "false Gospel" (Gal 1:6–8).

"The Antichrist" may not be an individual or even a single institution but a principle at work throughout this time between Christ's ministry and his second coming. Therefore the identification by the reformers of the papacy as "Antichrist" should not be construed as though this was a claim that every individual pope in history was an unbeliever—even less that every individual Roman Catholic is a non-Christian.

At least a partial parallel to this might be seen in the American expression "working for the Man." When someone speaks this way, "the Man" refers not to any individual or even to any single institution but rather to a representative authority—the boss. In this example, "the Man" could perhaps be defined as the corrupt use of power for the exploitation of others. In a somewhat similar way "the Antichrist" manifests itself variously, when religion and power are used so that they attempt to draw others away from the truth into destructive error. Thus, "Antichrist" has manifested itself in many times and places throughout history, such as Antiochus Epiphanes and his assault on the Jerusalem temple, the Roman emperor cult, the false teachings of the Renaissance papacy, and Islam.

The Reformers on the Topic of Antichrist

Various Church Fathers believed the Antichrist would be a successor to the Roman Empire. During the medieval period, some Franciscans and other theologians asserted strongly that the pope was the Antichrist. For example, John Hus wrote,

> As for antichrist occupying the papal chair, it is evident that a pope living contrary to Christ, like any other perverted person, is called by common consent antichrist. In accordance with [1] John 2:2, many are become antichrists. And the faithful will not dare to deny persistently that it is possible for the man of sin to sit in the holy place. (*Church* 128)

Others medieval Fathers saw the coming of the Antichrist in the attacks of the Muslim Turks.

The Lutheran Confessions describe papal and Islamic doctrines as "marks of Antichrist" and express the conviction that the Antichrist will manifest himself as an authority over the Church at the end of time. The Confessions' identification of the papacy as a manifestation of Antichrist has to do with official papal pronouncements that (1) condemn the teaching that we are justified before God by grace through faith in Christ without the works of the law and (2) the papal claim that it is necessary for salvation to be subject to the pope (Council of Trent, canons 9, 11, 12, 24; the papal decree *Unum Sanctum*). Melanchthon wrote, "The marks of Antichrist plainly agree with the kingdom of the pope and his followers. . . . [Paul] is not speaking about heathen kings, but about someone ruling in the Church" (Tr 39). Elsewhere he wrote,

> "And what need is there of words on a subject so manifest? If the adversaries defend these human services as meriting justification, grace, and the remission of sins, they simply establish the kingdom of Antichrist. For the kingdom of Antichrist is a new service of God, devised by human authority rejecting Christ, just as the kingdom of Mahomet has services and works through which it wishes to be justified before God; nor does it hold that men are gratuitously justified before God by faith, for Christ's sake. Thus

the Papacy also will be a part of the kingdom of Antichrist if it thus defends human services as justifying" (Ap XV, 18).

Luther likewise saw this prophecy fulfilling itself in the corruption of the church officials: "God's temple is not the description for a pile of stones, but for the holy Christendom (1Co 3[:17]), in which [the Antichrist] is to reign" (LW 40:232). Luther also wrote,

> "This teaching shows forcefully that the Pope is the very Antichrist, who has exalted himself above, and opposed himself against Christ because he will not permit Christians to be saved without his power, which, nevertheless, is nothing, and is neither ordained nor commanded by God" (SA, II, IV, 10).

Luther also commented on the role of Islam when he wrote,

> "Thus this Christian Church is physically dispersed among pope, Turks, Persians, Tartars, but spiritually gathered in one gospel and faith under one head, i.e. Jesus Christ. For the papacy is assuredly the true realm of Antichrist, the real anti-Christian tyrant, who sits in the temple of God and rules with human commandments, as Christ in Matthew 24[:24] and Paul in 2 Thessalonians 2[:3f.] declare; although the Turk and all heresies, wherever they may be, are also included in this abomination which according to prophecy will stand in the holy place, but are not to be compared to the papacy" (LW 37:367–368).

Hus, Melanchthon, and Luther were not alone in their views. Cranmer wrote freely about the papacy as the Antichrist. (See *The Remains of Thomas Cranmer, D. D. Archbishop of Canterbury*, Henry Jenkyns, ed., Vol. III (Oxford: Oxford University Press, 1833). The following passage from Calvin demonstrates similar concerns:

> My readers now understand, that all the sects by which the Church has been lessened from the beginning, have been so many streams of revolt which began to draw away the water from the right course, but that the sect of Mahomet was like a violent bursting forth of water, that took away about the half of the Church by its violence. It remained, also, that Antichrist should infect the remaining part with his poison. Thus, we see with our own eyes, that this memorable prediction of Paul has been confirmed by the event. . . . Now, every one that has learned from Scripture what are the things that more especially belong to God, and will, on the other hand, observe what the Pope claims for

himself . . . will have no great difficulty recognizing the Antichrist. (Calvin 328–29)

The medieval Fathers and the reformers wrote their comments in eras of persecution and corruption. Christians today may praise God that the tensions of those times have given way to better relations between Christians, especially following the Roman Catholic Church's Vatican II Council. It remains to be seen how Paul's prophecy about the man of lawlessness will be fulfilled. In the meantime, the earlier warnings about corrupt religious leadership serving Satan's purposes remain relevant.

2:6 *what is restraining him.* The man of lawlessness is confronted with an obstacle, a restrainer. Paul did not plainly write what this restraint was, though he had explained it to the Thessalonians (cf. Dn 9–11, especially 10; Rv 9:11–21). Various interpreters have suggested potential restrainers such as the Roman Empire, apostolic mission work, the rule of law, the Holy Spirit, or the Church. Since Paul did not provide a specific answer or further details, all such suggestions fail to satisfy. We will need to wait and see what Paul had in view. Until then, we may cling confidently to God's Word, which is our great comfort and help in every trial. *now.* The principle of the "man of lawlessness" ("the Antichrist") was already present in NT times (compare "already" in v. 7). See 1Jn 2:18–27.

2:7 *mystery of lawlessness.* See the note at v. 3. *he.* The restrainer. See the note at v. 6.

2:8 *breath.* This refers to the Word of Christ, of which the Holy Spirit is the preeminent preacher. This identification is supported by the fact that the Greek word used here, *pneuma*, means both "breath" and "Spirit/spirit" (cf. Eph 6:17). *appearance of His coming.* After the son of destruction is revealed, Jesus will destroy this lawless one and his evil deeds by the Word. This occurs with Christ's second coming. However, we are not told any dates or intervals of time regarding these climactic events.

2:9 *activity of Satan.* The lawless one is to be distinguished from Satan, yet he is an agent of Satan, while at the same time embodying and fully representing the evil that Satan is. Note the unholy anti-Trinity of Rv 13:1–18 (the dragon, which is Satan, the beast from the sea, which depicts corrupt political or other earthly power, and the beast from the land, which symbolizes false religion). This unholy alliance shows that "Antichrist" will manifest itself in multiple ways (see note, v. 3). *false signs and wonders.* This phenomenon is a parody by the Antichrist of the true Christ, who did true "mighty works and wonders and signs" (Ac 2:22). Jesus prophesied about this work of the devil (Mk 13:22–23). These evil and misleading miracles are intended to draw people into falsehood. Manifestations of "Antichrist" through history have often claimed miraculous deeds.

2:10 *love the truth and so be saved.* This refers to love of true doctrine, love of all that Jesus has commanded to be taught (Mt 28:19–20). Such love is not distinct from faith in Jesus; in fact, faith cherishes the truth (cf. Jn 8:31–32).

2:11 *God sends them a strong delusion.* God gives the perishing (those who unrepentantly persistent in unbelief; cf. Ps 14:1) over to the evil they themselves have chosen. If they persist in error, He gives them finally to evil's destructive end: condemnation. For example, through the prophet Amos, God spoke of how He may send a famine of hearing His Word upon those who had repeatedly disbelieved His Word. Furthermore, Pharaoh (Ex 8:15; 9:12) is an example of God giving someone who persisted in unbelief over to the inevitable consequences of that unbelief. This is a work of His Law (sometimes called God's "alien work"), but it is not what God desires for people. Cf. Rm 1:21–28; 11:8; 2Co 4:4; Rv 3:16. See also the following note.

2:12 *in order that all may be condemned.* God predestines/elects no one to condemnation; this would be counter to His very character and being as the God of grace and mercy in Christ Jesus (Ezk 33:11; 1Tm 2:3–4; cf. Jn 3:17–21; 2Pt 3:9; see further the notes at 2:13 and 2:14).

In the early years of the Reformation, Augustine influenced Luther on this topic. (Cf. his treatise on *The Bondage of the Will.*) However, after careful study of Scripture, Luther emphasized more and more God's desire to save all people. Luther stated that the reason God created us was to redeem us! (See quote under note at 1:12.) In contrast, Calvin took the teaching of Augustine in a different direction and taught that God elected some people for damnation. Melanchthon reacted sharply to Calvin's conclusions, regarding such views of election as a new form of Greek Stoicism. He affirmed that condemnation is truly self-chosen by willful rejection of God's love in Christ. See also the previous note.

2:1–12 in Devotion and Prayer Paul warned the Thessalonians not to be misled regarding the second coming of Christ, as though the day of the Lord had already come. He described those apocalyptic events yet to take place before the return of Jesus, specifically the revelation of the man of lawlessness. We must be on guard against deception. There is much false teaching, especially regarding the end times. Our only protection against falsehood is to cling to the Word of God: read the Bible, pray based on the Word, and continue to hear the Word in the communion of saints. The Lord, the Word made flesh, brings us life under this Word of truth. Paul pastorally comforts the Thessalonians, and us, that Christ will overthrow this Antichrist.

We look forward, with great hope and joy, to Christ's return in glory. • "Lord, keep us steadfast in Your Word; Curb those who by deceit or sword Would wrest the kingdom from Your Son And bring to naught all He has done. O Comforter of priceless worth, Send peace and unity on earth; Support us in our final strife And lead us out of death to life." Amen. (*LSB* 655:1, 3)

Encouragement and Thanksgiving (2:13–17)

ESV	KJV
¹³But we ought always to give thanks to God for you, brothers beloved by the Lord, because God chose you as the firstfruits to be saved, through sanctification by the Spirit and belief in the truth. ¹⁴To this he called you through our gospel, so that you may obtain the glory of our Lord Jesus Christ. ¹⁵So then, brothers, stand firm and hold to the traditions that you were taught by us, either by our spoken word or by our letter. ¹⁶Now may our Lord Jesus Christ himself, and God our Father, who loved us and gave us eternal comfort and good hope through grace, ¹⁷comfort your hearts and establish them in every good work and word.	¹³But we are bound to give thanks alway to God for you, brethren beloved of the Lord, because God hath from the beginning chosen you to salvation through sanctification of the Spirit and belief of the truth: ¹⁴Whereunto he called you by our gospel, to the obtaining of the glory of our Lord Jesus Christ. ¹⁵Therefore, brethren, stand fast, and hold the traditions which ye have been taught, whether by word, or our epistle. ¹⁶Now our Lord Jesus Christ himself, and God, even our Father, which hath loved us, and hath given us everlasting consolation and good hope through grace, ¹⁷Comfort your hearts, and stablish you in every good word and work.

Introduction to 2:13–17 These are profound and powerful words of encouragement regarding our salvation. This is one of the portions of Scripture that reveals to us that doctrine known as "the election of grace." This portion of the letter makes it plain that what is taught here is designed to be of great reassurance to believers.

2:13 *brothers beloved*. "Brother" is a common NT term for a fellow believer in Jesus Christ; "sister" (1Co 9:5) and "father" (1Co 4:15) could be used in a similar way. "Christian" would be a synonym. With such language the Scriptures depict Christians as members of the family of God, who are loved by the Lord Jesus. See note, Col

1:2. *chose you.* The Lord had the Thessalonian believers on His heart from eternity, a mystery of the faith that is of great comfort when facing times of persecution as the Thessalonians did. As we examine those passages that speak of God's choice, we are reassured regarding the certainty of salvation. Our salvation is entirely the work of God and does not depend on anything meritorious on our part. Furthermore, we are told that in fact God chose us for this salvation from all eternity (cf. Rm 8:29–39; Eph 1:3–14; 2Tm 1:9).

as the firstfruits. A number of Greek manuscripts read "from the beginning" (so KJV); this seems to fit better with the overall message of the passage and is in harmony with the Scriptural truth that God the Father chose us in Christ before He made the universe (cf. Eph 1:4; Rv 13:8). God chose the Thessalonians with the purpose, not only of saving them by His grace, but of reaching others with the gracious message of the Gospel. Since they were the firstfruits, more were to follow. *to be saved through sanctification by the Spirit and belief.* See the notes at 1:3, 11. The Holy Spirit, working through the Gospel of Christ (see following verse) calls us to saving faith in Christ. Through this faith our unholiness is forgiven. In this way the Spirit sanctifies us, that is, makes us holy before God. *in the truth.* Saving faith has a definite (and true) content, the Gospel (v. 14).

2:14 *our gospel.* This is the message of the work of Christ (1Co 15:1–4); it has the power of salvation (Rm 1:16). It is the means through which the Holy Spirit calls us to saving faith in Christ, through which we receive the salvation for which we were chosen. See also the note at 1:8. *obtain the glory.* See the note at 1:10.

2:15 *traditions.* We may tend to hear this word as designating something beyond or even contrary to the Scriptures (such would be the meaning of the word in a passage such as Mk 7:3). However, the Greek term designates "that which is given over," and in the Bible itself the term often denotes the true and authoritative teachings that are given over by God and Christ (such as through our Lord's apostles). Hence, in a passage such as this one the translation "doctrines" might more easily communicate the correct meaning. Even before any of the books of the NT were written, there was an established body of Christian teaching that one was not allowed to alter (cf. Ac 2:42). For example, in 1Co Paul alluded to basic Christian doctrines he had previously taught his readers (3:2, 16; 4:17; 6:9, 15–16; 9:13;

11:2, 23; 15:1, 3). In the present passage, the plural "traditions" would point to a number of doctrines. Gerhard wrote,

> The word "traditions" here is taken generally and is understood as all the teaching in whatever way it is handed down, either in speech or in writing. The apostle admonishes the Thessalonians to persevere constantly in the heavenly doctrine that he had handed down to them orally at that time, as well as that which he had begun to put into writing in this Epistle, as the connection of the apostolic text shows [vv. 5, 14–5]. (Gerhard E 1.405)

that you were taught. Paul meant the entirety of God's Word (see also Mt 28:19). *letter.* This refers to 1Th or to the present Letter or perhaps to both. At any rate the apostle was pointing to the authoritative nature of his Letters as being on a par with the inspired Scriptures of the OT; see further the note at Col 4:16.

2:16 *comfort.* The Greek term is *paraklesis*, an allusion to one of the Holy Spirit's names: the Comforter (KJV), Helper (ESV), or Paraclete (Jn 14:26). See further the note at 1Th 4:18. This term, along with the context (the Father, the Lord Jesus Christ, and the Holy Spirit are all mentioned in 2:13), makes the present blessing Trinitarian. *hope through grace.* Because of God's good favor toward us, His loving and kind disposition, we have sure hope for the day of redemption. See also the note at 3:16.

2:17 *hearts.* See the note at Col 2:2. *them.* Their hearts; a word supplied by the translators to provide an object for the verb "establish." The KJV tradition provided "you" (the Thessalonians) as the object of the verb. *work and word.* The Christian life involves both work (service to God and others) and word (proclamation, witness, and all wholesome use of our speech). See the note at Col 4:6.

2:13–17 in Devotion and Prayer Paul calls on the Thessalonians to stand firm in the faith the Lord has given them. He reminds them that both their calling and comfort have God as the source. We must not seek the truth in the spirit of the age, in the fads, trends, or ideas of today's marketplace. The God who has elected us unto salvation keeps us steadfast in the faith (cf. 1Th 5:23–24). The doctrine of election is a doctrine of the Gospel, by which we know that our salvation is guaranteed (Eph 1:14) because it depends on God alone, as He has chosen us before the foundation of the world (see also Rm 8:28; 9:11). God assures us of this through the external signs of His Word and Sacrament He handed down to us through the apostles.

• Lord, I praise You that by grace alone You chose me in Christ Jesus and have called me through the Gospel and Sacraments. As the Thessalonians were firstfruits of the Gospel, make me a fruitful witness of Your surpassing grace in Christ Jesus our only Savior. Amen.

PART 3

APOSTOLIC COMMANDS (3:1–15)

Request for Prayers (3:1–5)

ESV	KJV
3 ¹Finally, brothers, pray for us, that the word of the Lord may speed ahead and be honored, as happened among you, ²and that we may be delivered from wicked and evil men. For not all have faith. ³But the Lord is faithful. He will establish you and guard you against the evil one. ⁴And we have confidence in the Lord about you, that you are doing and will do the things that we command. ⁵May the Lord direct your hearts to the love of God and to the steadfastness of Christ.	3 ¹Finally, brethren, pray for us, that the word of the Lord may have free course, and be glorified, even as it is with you: ²And that we may be delivered from unreasonable and wicked men: for all men have not faith. ³But the Lord is faithful, who shall stablish you, and keep you from evil. ⁴And we have confidence in the Lord touching you, that ye both do and will do the things which we command you. ⁵And the Lord direct your hearts into the love of God, and into the patient waiting for Christ.

Introduction to 3:1–5 Among the instructions that Paul gave in the last sections of this Letter (3:6–18) are some that would be strong and challenging for the Thessalonians. After planting and caring for numerous congregations throughout Asia Minor and Greece, Paul understood that these new believers would struggle. He even anticipated what those struggles might be. Therefore, before turning to these challenges, the apostle began with more fraternal blessings and requests for prayer.

3:1 Paul requested intercessory prayer for the proclamation of the Gospel, particularly among those who as of yet do not have saving faith (cf. Eph 6:18–19; Col 4:3; 1Th 5:25). How easy it is for a congregation to become focused on internal concerns and lose

165

track of the focused mission that Jesus gave to the apostles and all believers: proclaim the Word of Christ. *honored.* This is Paul's way of saying that the message of Christ would be received through faith. Luther wrote,

> "We pray that His name may be so praised through God's holy Word and a Christian life that we who have accepted it may abide and daily grow in it, and that it may gain approval and acceptance among other people. We pray that it may go forth with power throughout the world" (LC III 52).

3:2 *wicked and evil men.* This could refer to persecutors of the congregation (1:6) or to false teachers, either within or outside the Christian Church (2Tm 2:17–18). Perhaps Paul had intentionally worded his Letter in such a way so as to include both. *not all have faith.* These words certainly could apply to all unbelievers. However, in this context the apostle was speaking both of the proclamation of the Gospel and of those who are wicked. He most likely had in mind those who are regarded as faithful or even profess to be faithful but actually deny the faith by their teachings or actions. This would include the Jews of that city who accepted the OT Scriptures but did not welcome the news that the OT prophecies were now fulfilled in Christ. Likewise, it may include those who were confusing or deceiving the Thessalonians about the coming of Jesus. See the note at 1:3. This passage also illustrates the truth that genuine faith is not something that people come by naturally. Of course, all people trust in someone or something, whether a religion, a philosophy, or even in themselves. But such "faith" is not the saving faith God advances in the name of Jesus Christ.

3:3 *faithful.* By a play on words with "faith" in the previous verse, Paul drew a sharp contrast between the enemies of the Gospel and the Christ of the Gospel. The Lord has shown Himself to be reliable and trustworthy. He has always kept His promises to His people (e.g., the exodus, the Promised Land, the Messiah) and will continue to keep them (cf. 1:6–7, 11–12; 2:8, 13–14). *guard you.* The apostle directed the Thessalonians and us to apostolic teaching ("the things that we command"; v. 4) and to "the love of God" and "the steadfastness of Christ" (v. 5). These are available to us in the means of grace (the Word, Baptism, and the Lord's Supper). *the evil one.* A reference to Satan (see also the notes at 2:3–4).

3:4 *we command.* The same term will recur in vv. 6, 10, and 12. Although Paul included his coworkers with him ("we"), he spoke here with the authority that was his as one called to be an apostle of Christ (see the note on apostle at Col 1:1). Today, such authority is exercised by those whom Christ calls into the apostolic Office of the Holy Ministry. The authority of ministers does not come from human power or influence. It has a spiritually binding basis, not one that comes from majority rule, the point of a sword, or human ordinances. The authority of ministers comes entirely from the Word of Christ and His Sacraments of Baptism and the Lord's Supper (See the notes at 1Th 5:12–13; see further Tr 60). Christ is the one working in and through the Office of the Ministry, using the man in it as an instrument of the Word (1Co 4:1). Melanchthon provided a similar insight in commenting on Heb 13:17 when he wrote, "This passage requires obedience to the Gospel. For it does not establish a dominion for the bishops apart from the Gospel" (Ap XXVIII 20).

3:5 *direct your hearts.* The Lord turns our hearts to Him. This brief request may slip past us without much notice. Yet think how often you have wanted to know God's will or purpose for your life, sought guidance in making a decision, or struggled to know what was most important for you and others. Here Paul held up a little compass for all such situations, pointing toward the love and steadfastness of the Lord. Although He is our anchor in the storms of life, He is ultimately our goal, the safe haven we seek in every circumstance. *hearts.* In biblical vocabulary this term refers to the total inner person; it indicates our communion with God through faith (cf. 2Pt 1:4). *steadfastness of Christ.* The steadfastness of Christ was displayed preeminently in His enduring death on a cross for the world's salvation (Php 2:8). In turn, His steadfastness for us becomes also the model for our life of solid devotion to Him (Php 2:5; cf. Heb 12:1–3). The following verses will point out how much the Thessalonians will need such steadfastness.

3:1–5 in Devotion and Prayer Paul requests prayer for his missionary work and obedience to what he has commanded them from the Word of God. We are called to listen to those whom God has given to teach and preach the pure Word (Heb 13:17; cf. Ac 5:27–32)—we listen with an ear for His teaching, which is why it is so important for all Christians to gain and retain a knowledge of the Holy Scripture. The Lord's faithfulness toward us is steadfast; He is an immovable rock. Yet He is also the soul's haven, our goal. Through the Church (His Body) and her pastors, He will guard us against the attacks of the evil one (the devil) and the Antichrist. • "Protect us from war, bloodshed, plagues, pestilence, and other grievous diseases. Guard us against all evil and distresses of the body. Let Your divine will, the growth of Your kingdom and the glory of Your name be accomplished in all these things. Amen." (Luther, *TLWA*, p. 336)

Discipline of the Disorderly (3:6–12)

ESV	KJV
⁶Now we command you, brothers, in the name of our Lord Jesus Christ, that you keep away from any brother who is walking in idleness and not in accord with the tradition that you received from us. ⁷For you yourselves know how you ought to imitate us, because we were not idle when we were with you, ⁸nor did we eat anyone's bread without paying for it, but with toil and labor we worked night and day, that we might not be a burden to any of you. ⁹It was not because we do not have that right, but to give you in ourselves an example to imitate. ¹⁰For even when we were with you, we would give you this command: If anyone is not willing to work, let him not eat. ¹¹For we hear that some among you walk in idleness, not busy at work, but busybodies. ¹²Now such persons we command and encourage in the Lord Jesus Christ to do their work quietly and to earn their own living.	⁶Now we command you, brethren, in the name of our Lord Jesus Christ, that ye withdraw yourselves from every brother that walketh disorderly, and not after the tradition which he received of us. ⁷For yourselves know how ye ought to follow us: for we behaved not ourselves disorderly among you; ⁸Neither did we eat any man's bread for nought; but wrought with labour and travail night and day, that we might not be chargeable to any of you: ⁹Not because we have not power, but to make ourselves an ensample unto you to follow us. ¹⁰For even when we were with you, this we commanded you, that if any would not work, neither should he eat. ¹¹For we hear that there are some which walk among you disorderly, working not at all, but are busybodies. ¹²Now them that are such we command and exhort by our Lord Jesus Christ, that with quietness they work, and eat their own bread.

Introduction to 3:6–15 Paul instructed his readers regarding their relationships with others who bear the name of "Christian." His sobering instruction here shows us that it may be necessary to withhold Christian fellowship from those who persist in error, doing so to bring them to repentance and to reformation in faith and/or life.

3:6 *we command.* See the note at v. 4. *in the name.* Cf. Ac 4:12. Paul had apostolic authority, which came from Christ Himself, and he reminded his hearers of this at the beginning of most of his Letters (cf. Gal 1:1). This is also a reminder that Christ has a claim on all who have been baptized into His name. *keep away.* Cf. vv. 14–15; Rm 16:17; 1Co 5:9–13. When the apostle directed his readers to "keep away from," to "avoid" (Rm 16:17), and to "have nothing to do with" (2Th 3:14) one who is or who at least claims to be a fellow Christian ("brother," see below), he did not mean that we are to shun any contact with such a one (1Co 5:9–10). Rather, he was speaking of withholding fellowship (expressed preeminently in joint corporate worship) with such a one. The similar circumstances at Corinth are instructive. Note the contrast between "purge the evil person from among you" (1Co 5:13, where "you" is plural) with "when you come together as a church" (1Co 11:18, cf. v. 20) to describe the congregation's services of Word and Sacrament. The goal of this withholding of fellowship was to cause the offending brother to turn from his erroneous doctrine and/or conduct (1Co 5:1–5; cf. 2Co 2:5–11). *brother.* See the note at 2:13. The instruction of this passage and similar ones applies not only with respect to non-Christians but even in regard to erring Christians. In either case, the goal is that the individual come to repentance and faith in the truth (cf. v. 15). *walking in idleness.* See also 1Th 4:11–12; 5:14. The specific problem at Thessalonica being addressed here is that some were neglecting their daily responsibilities and common tasks and meddling in the affairs of others. Perhaps this was because they anticipated that the end of the world was imminent (2:1–3), or perhaps they were simply lazy and arrogant (cf. v. 11). Bengel wrote,

> He keeps the Thessalonians in suspense, until at ver. 11 he brings out the matter, at which he was aiming. They seem to have given up labour on account of the near approach of the day of Christ. The admonitions of the first epistle were more gentle; in the second, there is now some degree of complaint, although that

complaint regards a slip of that kind which only tempts minds of high (spiritual) attainments. (Bengel 235)

the tradition that you received. This refers to the standard according to which all such situations are to be decided, namely, the written Word of God (note the occurrence of "letter" in the similar directive of 3:14, and see the fuller note at 2:15). Thus, "the tradition that you received" would include apostolic teaching and instruction regarding both Christian doctrine and Christian conduct; the Holy Spirit inspired men to record this for us in the NT.

3:7 *imitate us.* This is a theme that occurred elsewhere in Paul's Letters; he called on his hearers to imitate him because he imitated Jesus (cf. 1Co 11:1; Eph 5:1–21). In this case, Paul reminded the Thessalonians that when Silvanus, Timothy, and he were with them, they were not idle, disorderly, or undisciplined, but they "worked night and day" (v. 8). See further the note on "walking in idleness" at v. 6.

3:8 Cf. 2Co 11:7. Although he had the God-given right to make a living from the Gospel (see the following note), it was Paul's usual custom to provide his own support through plying his trade as a tentmaker; cf. Ac 18:1–3.

3:9 *have that right.* See the previous note; see also 1Co 9:14–15a; Gal 6:6; 1Tm 5:17–18. Calvin wrote,

As Paul wished by his laboring to set an example, that idle persons might not like drones eat the bread of others, so he was not willing that this very thing should do injury to the ministers of the word, so that the Churches should defraud them of their proper livelihood. . . . There was a danger, lest the Thessalonians, having had from the beginning the preaching of the gospel from Paul's mouth gratuitously, should lay it down as a law for the future as to other ministers. (Calvin 354)

an example to imitate. See the note at v. 7.

3:10 *this command.* See the note at v. 4. *anyone is not willing to work, let him not eat.* This has been called "the Golden Rule of work." It is related to both the general and specific instructions already given orally and in writing, especially the command given in v. 6. A careful translation of the Greek ("if anyone is not willing to work") makes it clear that Paul was not disdaining compassionate charity for those in need but was speaking here of those who can provide for themselves but who neglect to do so. One of the ways that Christianity wholesomely influenced the culture around it was by giving dignity to manual labor (Eph 4:28; see further the note at Col 3:22).

3:11 *we hear.* Paul did not identify from whom or how he had heard this news, though perhaps it was through the person who had delivered 1Th. *busybodies.* The ESV translation ("not busy at work, but busybodies") brings out the play on words that is present in the original Greek. See further the note on "walking in idleness" at v. 6. The early Christian document known as the Didache says, "See to it that, as a Christian, he shall not live with you idle. But if he wills not so to do, he is a Christ-monger. Watch that you keep aloof from such" (*ANF* 7:381).

3:12 *command.* See the note at v. 4. *quietly.* Perhaps "as is in keeping with what is proper" would capture the idea of this word. The apostle instructed his readers to work without interfering in the work of others and without arrogantly seeking to draw attention to themselves (cf. vv. 6, 11). Paul offered similar instruction on conducting one's self "quietly" in 1Th 4:11; see further the note on that verse.

Admonition to Do Good (3:13–15)

ESV	KJV
¹³As for you, brothers, do not grow weary in doing good. ¹⁴If anyone does not obey what we say in this letter, take note of that person, and have nothing to do with him, that he may be ashamed. ¹⁵Do not regard him as an enemy, but warn him as a brother.	¹³But ye, brethren, be not weary in well doing. ¹⁴And if any man obey not our word by this epistle, note that man, and have no company with him, that he may be ashamed. ¹⁵Yet count him not as an enemy, but admonish him as a brother.

3:14 *have nothing to do with him.* See the note at 3:6.

3:15 It is at times necessary, and indeed truly loving, for one believer to speak the word of the Law to another in order to bring that person to see the harmful evil of his or her ways and to repent. See the fuller note at v. 6. Calvin wrote,

> Excommunication is distinguished from anathema: for as to those that the Church marks out by the severity of its censure, Paul admonishes that they should not be utterly cast away, as if they were cut off from all hope of salvation; but endeavours must be

used, that they may be brought back to a sound mind. (Calvin 361)

3:6–15 in Devotion and Prayer Those who persist in error, such as those who are idle, are to be avoided and even denied fellowship in order that this might cause them to repent, amend their ways, and return to their fellow believers. Laziness is a serious sin against the God who created us and gave us talents and abilities. It is a sin against the Body of Christ, against our brothers and sisters in the Lord, to whom we have been joined and with whom we are to be co-workers. The good news is that this word of the condemning Law is not the last word. The Law shows us our need for the Savior from sin; the Gospel gives us that Savior. • Heavenly Father, I thank You that in Baptism You have broken into my life, unified me with the life of Christ, and chosen me for citizenship in Your kingdom. I praise You for this inheritance, this home, this family. I bless You for never having forgotten me and never ceasing to yearn for me, to seek me, to call me, to offer me forgiveness anew. Amen.

PART 4

CONCLUSION (3:16–18)

Prayer for Peace (3:16)

ESV	KJV
¹⁶Now may the Lord of peace himself give you peace at all times in every way. The Lord be with you all.	¹⁶Now the Lord of peace himself give you peace always by all means. The Lord be with you all.

Introduction to 3:16–18 Although this conclusion to the Letter is brief, it contains some weighty words of reassurance for the readers.

3:16 *The Lord be with you all.* This ancient Israelite greeting (Ru 2:4) underscored God's promise to abide with His people (Is 7:14; Mt 1:23; cf. Mt 28:20). This is a liturgical benediction and confident prayer that the Lord is indeed with them and will continue to be so. See the notes at 1:2 and 2:16. The liturgical nature of such blessings is in keeping with the fact that the apostle intended his Letters to be read aloud publicly, in the context of corporate worship. See Col 4:16 and note.

Greeting (3:17)

ESV	KJV
¹⁷I, Paul, write this greeting with my own hand. This is the sign of genuineness in every letter of mine; it is the way I write.	¹⁷The salutation of Paul with mine own hand, which is the token in every epistle: so I write.

3:17 *own hand.* Paul had, in his usual manner, been dictating while someone else wrote. Then he wrote the conclusion in his own hand, a common practice in ancient letter writing. Paul knew that he had been wrongly cited for support in the spread of false teaching (2Th 2:2). His greeting in his own hand is a guarantee that this Letter really comes from him. See Col 4:18 and the note there; see also Gal 6:11; Phm 19.

Benediction (3:18)

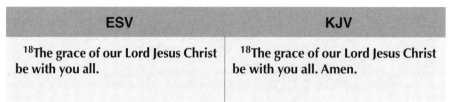

ESV	KJV
¹⁸The grace of our Lord Jesus Christ be with you all.	¹⁸The grace of our Lord Jesus Christ be with you all. Amen.

3:18 Compare this blessing with that of v. 16 and see the note there. *grace.* Paul closed this Letter with "grace," just as he opened it (1:2); see the note at Col 4:18. On the addition of "Amen," see note, Col 4:18.

3:16–18 Paul concluded his Letter with a prayer for peace and, in his own hand, a blessing of grace. We should imitate Paul in his blessing. We should pray for peace for others, even for our enemies. We should bless, and not curse, even those we do not like, even those who do us harm (Rm 12:19; 1Pt 3:9). Our prayer for God's peace and grace in our lives is no mere wish. We do have peace with God and with one another through the blood of Christ; by the grace of our Lord, this is a peace that passes all understanding and remains steadfast regardless of external assaults by the devil (cf. Eph 2:11–21; Col 1:19–20; Jn 14:27). • "O God, from whom come all holy desires, all good counsels, and all just works, give to us, Your servants, that peace which the world cannot give, that our hearts may be set to obey Your commandments and also that we, being defended from the fear of our enemies, may live in peace and quietness; through Jesus Christ, Your Son, our Lord, who lives and reigns with You and the Holy Spirit, one God, now and forever." Amen. (*LSB*, p 233)